The Dawning of The Dove

Humbly, Simply, Unadorned

Arrives the Promise of the Future

By Rae Lundstrom

Sacred Writer, Spiritual Teacher

Rae Lundstrom

The Dawning of The Dove

The Dawning of The Dove speaks of Spiritual Truth, Divine Love. What is it that we are seeking at this time? Why now? When? How?

The Dawning of The Dove beckons our soul's evolution to a higher state of consciousness. Why this is a crucial part of our evolution where every human is an active participant.

The planetary evolution of the Great Mother Earth, Gaia -- What does this mean to humanity? How do we work with Earth? What is it she is asking of us? What is actually happening within her Soul Consciousness?

The language used as interpreted by the reader will speak to them to grasp its significance on a very deep core level.

The Dawning of The Dove encourages people to genuinely look at their beliefs and realize they have a choice. Does humanity realize how crucial their choice is collectively and individually? Ultimately, the journey begins and ends within the HU-MAN!

The Dawning of The Dove is such a book

Copyright © 2002 Rae Lundstrom

ISBN 13: 979-8-4155-9641-6

This book is dedicated to the glorious children of God...

that they may see who they are,

believe and trust in them,

and trust in God's Love for them!

Dear Friends of The Dawning of The Dove,

I was very delighted when my friend and colleague, Rae Lundstrom, asked me to share my personal experience as part of her own inspirational story.

May we forever walk in the light of peace, love and blessings.

The Dawn of The Dove

The tragedy of 9/11 had taken place and laid heavily on my heart and mind.

The Sunday morning following, I awoke saying "the dawn of the dove." As I sat up, I repeated the phrase. What did it mean? The dove is a sign of peace, so did it mean the beginning of a new era of peace in the world? How did that phraseology come about?

I sought spiritual counsel and learned that in slumber I had been conversing with and questioning a powerful guide about 9/11 and was informed that 9/11 had to happen before the world can live in peace. It is the dawn of a new age that we have been waiting for. The era is approaching.

The guide then said, "Remember, this is the dawn of the dove." That phrase was what I had picked up on and had awakened repeating it, which pleased him very much.

What a mystical gift! I was highly honored.

- Betty Spain Edwards RScP

The Author

SACRED WRITER, SPIRITUAL TEACHER

RAE LUNDSTROM, RScP is a Licensed Spiritual Practitioner with twenty years of service counseling people of all ages in their personal challenges ranging from relationship conflicts, health, aging, to death and dying, and resolving life's situations. She is a strong leader in support groups as a licensed Practitioner.

Rae is a gifted spiritual healer on many levels being educated in Holistic Health and the Healing Arts. She received her training from The Upledger Institute, Inc. in CranioSacral Therapy (CST) and Lymph Drainage Therapy followed by additional training from the Western Colorado Center for Cranio- Sacral Treatment. She has trained in other modalities of healing and energy work, which is also a part of her practice. Using her unique gifts and intuitive wisdom she has helped many to heal on a mind, body, and soul level. "Healing" is a natural ability Rae has, including that of just her 'Presence.'

Amidst her broad repertoire, she is a clear and dynamic facilitator and communicator known for building strong relationships across a diverse background. Her entrepreneurial leadership led her to establishing her own import/distribution company successfully marketing and introducing her company and products throughout the United States and Canada.

As an entrepreneur she is experienced in many areas. Trade shows experience on both that of the attendee and participant. Event sponsorship, sales and marketing coupled with public speaking.

Today, she is a skilled speaker, lecturer and presenter who has facilitated many workshops, Her favorite is when she is presenting "Stories of Hope, with Rae" and that of her "Angel Voices". She is no stranger to public speaking and loves to be in front of an audience.

She is an author writing specifically pertaining to Spiritual wisdom in relationship to her own personal experience with the Angelic realms and that of Spirit.

After experiencing a Spiritual Awakening, Rae discovered the greater part of "Who I Am." and enlightenment. She has authored her God-inspired book "The Dawning of The Dove", which serves to assist humanity at this time of much speculation of the coming times. The book offers hope and faith through all adversities through that of God and His Divine Plan for us.

Rae chooses to serve God and mankind at this critical juncture on our planet Earth through a better understanding of what is transpiring and why, confirming that of our Divinity and remembering God is in Charge and His Hand is in everything!

Rae invites you to join her in this Grand Adventure of Spirit as these exciting times unfold.

CONTENTS

MEDITATION

____

Blessed Father-Mother God,

As Earth transforms herself out of the darkness and

as we transform ourselves,

we ask that the Christed Light surround our

souls, penetrating all spheres and levels of consciousness, and bless

our souls with inner peace.

Through the love of the Christ that is the unification of all things,

we reach to expand that which is

ALL.

Preface

Beloveds:

There are undoubtedly many who will ask of me how this book came to

I ask this of myself often. I am a divorcee, mother, and businesswoman.

I am a Licensed Spiritual Practitioner, serving God and humanity in my so doing. I find my life very much engrained in every day circumstances, necessities, distractions, and requirements of today's lifestyle. Indeed, this is my life as I have created it while also seeking to live in a simpler manner, as many would have it for themselves today.

For all appearances, mine appears to be a very normal life.

However, below the surface, I kept a constant vigil to learn and know more regarding my own spirituality, my own truth. I was continually seeking, studying, and attending workshops and classes. I questioned. After a time of much soul searching and spiritual experiences, there awakened a part of my- self that I was not acquainted with—or, perhaps, I had chosen to secret away or hide from. Through my awakening, the seed was planted and I became resilient in the pursuit of finding the greater part of *who I am*.

I followed the richness of my soul's desire for me to experience Spirit in many enchanting and extraordinary ways, enticing me ever forward in my spiritual growth and advancement. I was on an adventure of such magnitude that it became overwhelming and I choose to remain silent regarding my spirituality—that is, until I was led, through meditation and prayer, to interpret what I experienced to be the Truth of which I had a profoundly deep "knowing and feeling."

Ultimately it was my soul, the essence of my being, cometh forth through my belief and my pen. Once begun, the flow was ceaseless, ever increasing in tempo, striving to complete that which I had undertaken. This flow of inspiration catapulted me forward to a place I had never expected or anticipated.

I was reluctant to share that which I had written, yet I knew it had a sense of urgency that compelled me to write and reveal.

Beloveds, may I present to you *The Dawning of the Dove*. May it serve as a means to escort you to the Throne of God, to assist in your entrance to His Kingdom.

I now bid you to read these pages in the purity of which they were written and to let its message speak to you as it will—or not, if the message has no relevance to you.

I ask that these words not induce fear but rather the Love of the God within as His splendor unfolds for the advancement of mankind at this time of planetary evolution.

God Is. I am. So it is!

—Rae Lundstrom

Spiritual Teacher, Sacred writer

As penned this day, September 20, 2002

Introduction

MY JOURNEY BEGINS

Now comes the time to write about the experience of what brought this Discourse to the fore. For many a year it has lain torment (there is no mistake in my writing this word for years I have tormented myself by not allowing my God-self to come forth and do my work for God) within my being, silently, patiently waiting, beckoning, an inner awareness lying dormant, yet ever so alive to yield to its burning fire to Be! To speak, write, share that of which I feel ever so deeply in my soul, bringing forth that which is my Truth!

This wellspring of my life bursts forth now! How does one write of one's soul's journey, to portray the window of your soul to the world? Indeed how? Humbly, I approach this with much trepidation for who am I that I can share with the world that of which I have borne witness to. It is with much joy, and love, I share with you this day that of which I hold close to my sacred heart and that of my boundless gratitude to that of the Heavenly Father, allowing for Divine Grace of our Creator God that lies within for which I AM eternally and forever One.

The year of the Lord was Two Thousand. I had been on my spiritual journey for some time, perhaps my whole life, unbeknownst to me. A beloved friend invited me to share and serve as my tour guide to travel to the Majestic Mountain of Mt. Shasta. Mt. Shasta is well known amidst the Spiritual com- munity for its magical lore and unearthly experiences. Little did I know what lay ahead of me.

In contrast to my friend, who had actually lived at the base of this great Mountain, I knew very little about it: thus, I was resistant and felt I had obligations and quite literally had no intention of going and replied "Well, if the angels want me to go, then it will all work out." Little did I know what was in store for my friend and me!

As the time approached, everything seemed to just fall into place.

Before I knew it both she and I were driving up the highway surrounded by the most beautiful countryside of green trees, meadows and beauty that was beholden unto the eyes to gaze upon. The azure blue sky and crystal snow- capped mountain beckoned us forward. Thus my story begins.

Grace (not her real name) had prepared me well. She had shared her deep, spiritual wisdom and other aspects of life, as well as her creative mind wanting the explanations of how our Universe works in depth, the biology of Earth and her sacred sights, ley lines and her search for the meaning of it all. I learned more from Grace then I ever could have from books, though she introduced me to some fascinating books and people along the way! Grace was the catalyst I had needed in my life to "really" wake me up!

Our first approach to the mountain was walking up a well-traveled trail leading us to a beautiful meadow full of colorful flowers with a stream running through it, appropriately named Panther Meadow. Loving water and nature as I do, I rushed over to see it. Losing my footing, or feeling rather pushed, I sat down rather abruptly at the edge of the stream. Grace and her longtime friend, Jane (also not her real name) laughed and said "I guess "they" want you to spend some time here!" So off they went to investigate another part of the trail. Alone, I was immediately drawn into the beautiful energy of the Mountain. In meditation I asked for purification of my embodiment and spirit, to be open to whatever this incredible place had for me.

When I arose, I walked along the trail and discovered an enormous rock that I immediately climbed upon and stretched out full length, basking in the warmth of the August sun.

I held a video in my hand, while in flight to Mt Shasta, of what was proposed to happen in California. I was so disturbed I wrote on a piece of paper "I am going to speak to God." Thus, I lay there talking to God and the Archangels, pure in spirit and my emotional self. I beseeched God as to WHY? I began to speak to Him about that for which I had come.

I questioned the time we were living in, why we were so challenged in this lifetime. What humanity was facing and our planet, we called home. I was terribly upset when I learned of the upcoming Earth changes and humanity living in a perilous time on the planet. I cried all the way as I viewed the coast- line of California, which was proposed to sink into the ocean. So distraught was I, it was the foremost thing on my mind…"What about the people, God? What about the people?"

By that time my friends had returned and prodded me to come along with them. I climbed down from my perch and continued on our exploration surrendering that of which I'd asked unto God. Grace had an extensive itinerary for us during out stay here. As my tour guide, she wanted me to experience, see and do everything in the area. Thus, I was introduced to the lovely community, its people and wonderful shops. Grace had been studying the "I Am" teaching for some time and was very familiar with the I AM Foundation located right there in Mt Shasta. Unfortunately, they were not open when we arrived. Not to be dismissed lightly, Grace had earlier introduced me to their teachings.

I was surprised to learn Grace had purchased tickets for that evening to the "I AM" Come! Pageant which was held only once a year and happened to be that particular weekend in Mt Shasta's great outdoor amphitheater.

Never having seen the Pageant, I was transfixed as I bore witness to the Life and Crucifixion-Resurrection of the Ascended Master Jesus. This replication of the Life of Master Jesus left me feeling to the core of my being an inner pulsation of familiarity which seemed to ring true in every cell in my body… *remember*! I carried this pulsation within my body while traversing this Great Mountain. It seemed to not want to leave me, though subdued with the agenda being followed; it lay below the surface ever present.

The next day, Grace and I ventured to another side of the Mountain where she wanted me to experience ley lines that were directly connected to Omaha, Nebraska. She wanted to prove to me what she knew. We climbed a very high and narrow trail on the side of the mountain, with other climbers ahead of and behind us. The trail became steeper and I began to feel light-headed, shifting my body up the side of the cliff clinging to the earth and any other thing I could hold onto. If we had gone any further I knew I would experience acrophobia. Finally we circled back and landed on the other side of the mountain. Both of us stopped for a minute to catch our breath and enjoy the view of the far off mountain ranges, far-reaching and yet so close. I asked, "Grace, will you stay here while I go over there on the side of mountain and sit down and meditate for a while." "OK" she stated. Unbeknownst to either of us, Grace was my "Panther" holding the space and grounding us both.

I sat down amidst some rocks enjoying the view from where I was perched. Allowing myself to relax into this Majestic Mountain's Being, I closed my eyes to meditate. Most of the details of what happened as I sat there in the silence are too personal to share in this book at this time. But I will tell what I can.

Instantly, and without forewarning, I was surrounded by an Essence of Pure Light. My Essence was being impulsed by that of God. An explanation was given to my questions, impulsed through me through God's Inner Light. I 'knew" that it was the Essence of Christ. The message was for the world, for humanity, and not for me alone, addressing the journey we are on. This journey is the expansion of the Universe, of Creation, to reach that of the Christ Consciousness and higher dimensions. As I experienced this essence of myself and that of the PURE ESSENCE OF GOD THE CHRIST there was nothing else encapsulated as I was in this CHRISTED LIGHT!

Coming to, awakening into my embodiment was a very strange experience in itself. I found myself sitting exactly as I had left my body. Empty though it must have been as I was totally out of my body for that time, there it sat…whole and complete. As I reentered it I experienced coming back into my human form, regaining my consciousness of this reality, spotting Grace where I had originally left her. I waved to her and said to give me a few minutes and I would get there.

Unsteady on my feet, I tried to stand up. It took a few minutes for me to get accumulated into my body, and as I headed over to meet Grace I was so electronically charged throughout my whole embodiment that I could not move. Fortunately, there was a tree before me and I clung to it for dear life, as the pulsation of electricity ran through me. I held my head against the tree and yelled to Grace…"I can't move … please wait for me. "

Grace then realized I had had an "experience" on Mt Shasta. What an understatement! Once I felt somewhat stable, we began to descend the Mountain. At one point, I stopped, and had an extraordinary feeling of transcendence…stopping in midstride, experiencing the ONENESS of everything… from a blade of grass to the entire Cosmos…how connected we are….all of us! Nothing will ever be the same as my view of the world/Cosmos is forever changed from illusion into ultimate Reality.

As we resumed our trip down the trail, a beautiful dragonfly appeared before us; Grace commented "Look, there is a dragonfly leading us down the trail." Sure enough, it led us all the way down to our car. We knew Dragonfly was Spirit guiding us down. Dragonfly is the power of Light, according to *Animal Speaks* by Ted Andrews.

Finally settled in Grace's car, my entire body began shaking, and I began to sob uncontrollably. Grace stopped the car, and asked me what I'd experienced. I could not share it with her at that time but rather could only hold it close to my heart and be with it … for it was beyond words to be conveyed. Grace stated I should immediately write down what I'd experienced because it is easily forgotten. I did not get to do so as we rejoined with the friends we were staying with. Even as I write this, I am not sure it is for the world to know, nor do I want to be out there, perhaps that is why I really waited so long.

Life has escaped me, and I let the moments come and go, while all the time within my heart lay this Great Tiding and I, through my narrow mindedness, fear, and human consciousness, chose to forgo what was given…until now, as time is running out. I choose to do the work, as I am a human being here to serve God, as do the Ascended Masters, Archangels and angels, Councils, and other planetary systems at this critical junction of life on Planet Earth and that of the Cosmos.

CHAPTER I

My Invitation

Most of civilization is shut down, unconscious and unaware, not willing to open itself up to anything that is different or of another thought or perspective. Many have been stuck for so long in fear and old tribal thinking that we don't know how to think in any other way.

That is because thinking is always within the old perimeters, the old thought patterns and consciousness, the old way of being and doing. But this old way will no longer serve society or civilization or the planet or any creature thereon. The old way is fast disappearing as the human race realizes we can no longer sustain life the way we have been acting, the way we have been operating, and the way we have destroyed life and sought to destroy even humanity itself!

God will not allow this! God will not allow His children to self-destruct either themselves or the planet. The human race and the planet are invaluable to both the Cosmos and our Creator.

God has bequeathed to each heart eternal Life and Love! Claim that Life, that Love. Be. Live the truth of who you are. Once and for all, accept the greatness of your Being for it is truly beautiful, more beautiful and magnificent than you can ever imagine!

"Seek," sayeth the Father, "and you shall find!" Can you not seek that part of yourself that longs to be recognized, longs to become the fuller part of who you are? It is the soul's journey in life that matters, not the personality or the outer ego, which are the parts we have been so mislead to believe make up who we truly are. But the truth is: The ego no longer serves us.

This is a time of great awakening with greater awareness than has ever transpired on the planet. This rise in consciousness was necessary to reach this point of transformation!

The transformation requires that each soul evaluate itself, to look at the deepest truth inside. What do you truly believe? What have you not looked at about yourself? What do you hide behind? Is it the Bible, the Church, the religions of mankind?

Tribal consciousness would have you believe there is only one way to find God. God would have you know there are many ways to His House, His Kingdom, not just the way of mankind that has been perpetuated for centuries on our planet. God is free and ever loving. He honors each of you, His beloved children on this planet, for who you are. He is a benevolent God, a God of great kindness!

Why then do you judge yourself or others so harshly? Come now; face your fears, face your doubts and grace yourself. See that within you is the light and love of all creation, all aspects of yourself both of light and of dark. It is all right to have both light and dark; we are *human* after all! If one could look at the dark within oneself, without judgments and condemnation it would no longer be necessary to project it outward. As we tend to judge one another, we hold that person back from ever moving forward. Come now; view yourself in the sweet innocence of your being, that sweet baby born unto your Father-Mother God! Realize that you are a sweet life force of energy here on Earth at this time to be one of the catalysts for this enormous change. This loving energy of the Divine, of which you are part, for there is no separation, will transport both you and Gaia forward to the heavenly place you desire to be.

Always we speak of "Heaven on Earth." Is that not what we have requested for over two thousand years? Is that not what we ask for now? "Ask and you shall receive" for God loves to give to His children what they ask!

So it is now. So it is at this time when we shall have our Heavenly Earth with Peace for One Thousand Years or more if we so choose. So it is, we shall experience all of whom we are, evolving into our truly magnificent species. Come now, children of the Light of God, behold His words for us this day, opening our hearts and allowing ourselves to receive God's Loving Energy.

We must know through our sacred heart, our soul's being, that we are Divine. We are of God. In this exalted state of our pure essence, our God-Self, we know from our sacred heart we are that! God's Sacred Heart beating to the rhythm of our sacred heart. His Sacred Heart-our sacred heart as One! There is no duality, no separation, for God is within us! Honor God as the "You" of you. God who breathes our every breath; *The Breath of Life*. The Great IS-ness of life. Nothing else matters! Once we grasp this "knowing- ness," how powerful our lives become transformed.

Come now, His Children, lay down your arms, rest this day releasing all the old judgments, the old ways of thinking and being. Let go, Surrender to God all that holds you bound to these old Earthly ways, all that holds you so tightly encrusted in the old premises. I invite you to join with me and examine those ways, beliefs, and truths. What are they really? How do they work for you now at this time of your life? Do guilt and fear and other negative emotions serve you now; If so how, and in what way? God wants you to know that you do not need to carry all this weight around with you one moment longer.

We have been led to believe for over two thousand years that our burden was to carry all of the guilt of Jesus' crucifixion. That event in the long-historical past was not our fault! Death and the fear of death are not our truth!

The Truth of the Cross is that Jesus has Risen! Jesus is Light and Truth. Even as we speak today, He remains that Light, that Truth! Jesus did not instill fear, hate, anger, guilt, or judgment as He walked among us and brought His message. Then, as now, the message is always the same: "Love yourself. Love one another. Love God." Be at peace within your heart and soul.

Be not afraid of that which goes on around you, for you and God are One. God is here! He will never leave you! Never! Not in the midst of chaos, pain, or transition. Remain steadfast within the chaos, offering Love and Light to the situation sending the Christed energy to assist with prayer and blessings. His greatest joy is to be with you through all things at all times!

You are never alone for God resides within. Call upon Him often that He guide you and show you the way. Be not ever in fear that you are not worthy, for you are His most beholden being on Earth, His beloved son and daughter, His life form. His energy as expressed through you because of who you are in all of your magnificent light and glory! And as you shine so does He Shine and His Heart is full with glory and joy.

Come now; walk with Him this day as you did then. Walk with Him and listen to His Words and those of all the other Ascended Masters who have come before. And know it is the same now as it was then. Know that nothing in Truth changes. This time you change, for now you hear the words differently, you hear what is really spoken. You know these words are true because you recognize the words and feelings associated with them are *Truth*. This *knowing* requires not a church, a religion, a school, or a means to pray with Him. Rather, be assured, He hears you always, every minute; ever minutely, ever softly, He is there to speak with you and spend time honoring your walk as you come forth into the true being of who you are! Thus you allow Him to be His True Self as well. You allow Him to walk once again upon the planes of the Earth, for through you all is co-created with God. It is through you that thought is formed and brought forth on our planet. It is God through you, as your conscious thought and feelings, that all things are made manifest and possible.

Do you see how profound this is? How powerful you are? How magnificent? You are not a mere soul; you are a Divine soul, and it is gifted to you that all things are possible! We are the creators of our own Reality. Free yourself from the stigma of lack, limitation, judgment, and evil. Free your heart. Open your entire being to the conscious awareness of God's possibilities and potentials for our life to view other perspectives whereby we can actually live our dreams.

It is quite a beautiful experience to open oneself up to joy and to your true Self, your soul—to experience the sacredness of life within all nature, all life, and the entire Cosmos of existence as it harmonizes within the perfect Oneness of the Divine. The more you believe and create from this energy of Oneness, of Love, from the heart center, the more it is possible to live in peace, harmony and joy and the manifestation of your desires.

Your belief brings forth whatever you desire to manifest through Spirit. Divine Law is always given to you as you believe. This is the way the universe is designed, as a Universal Principle, which operates throughout everything and all life everywhere. God abides by your belief; there is no other way! This must be so because God, as God, cannot possibly force a belief on you until you are ready to create and formulate your Divine beliefs within yourself.

God merely asks you to understand that your worthiness is of utmost importance for, without your belief in yourself, nothing can be given to you.

Even this fact is, again, given to you as you believe: If you believe you are unworthy, there is no opening, no possible way that God can bring forth all that He has for you. If you are not open to receive all that which He delights in giving you, then it's like you have built an impenetrable wall between you and your Divine Self. The bigger and thicker the wall ("the belief"), the more difficult it is for your human self to see or experience anything else, for the wall is always there! Remove the wall and suddenly you will realize a space, a free flowing area of Light that can allow new energy to emerge and bring forth new experiences.

Humanity has been dictated to for centuries regarding our unworthiness, guilt, and fears. We have been judged so very deeply that our own conscious- ness has meshed with these conditional thoughts, and there is no end to the merciless of it all. Even today in our great society, per se, we are enmeshed in this old energy that has been brought forth for centuries to keep humanity down and controlled. There are many who would wish to further control us by instilling the same beliefs we, and our ancestors, have heard and lived with for so many lifetimes. Humanity is now awakening to this great deception realizing what is true and what is not. Now is the time when all that is not of truth, operating through manipulation and fear, will be made known and unable to withstand the new energy here on Earth. So it is the time now to reevaluate your own personal truths—your beliefs, if you will—and come to really know if they are yours or from someone else's belief system, perhaps your parents, a loved one or of a tribe or society/culture.

Explore your inner being and discover: What is revealed to you as to where and how you came across that belief? Is it yours? Was it ever? What would you be able to do, accomplish, or be without this belief holding you back all this lifetime, leaving you to be free in your wholeness of Spirit?

Regardless of the answers you uncover and regardless of the source, thank that source for caring enough about you to attempt to guide you. And, then, let the old thoughts and feelings go, forgiving yourself and whomever and whatever circumstances sending loving energy of your Christ-Self, of the Divine to cleanse, purge and release it forever.

Instead, come now and seek your own truth. Do not be afraid. Open your sacred heart and soul to the person you were designed to be. Relish this experience of life as God's greatest gift!

Life is the great teacher in Earth's classroom. Is it not time to *be*? Just *be* and nothing else!

Walk with me now and enjoy the freedom this truth brings to you, the enlightenment of your soul in complete unlimited freedom with your God-Self! What discoveries do you find? What hidden agendas do you have? What lights up your heart, your eyes, and smile that is the grander part of you?

When you are so bound by the belief that there is only one small part of you, the other potentials go unseen. The thoughts and feelings that you are unworthy or your life does not matter is a reflection on your Creator; He who stated, "You are created in the Image and Likeness of God." Consequently, you limit yourself and, thus, remain in old paradigm and energy patterns, not growing and moving forward to discover all the other aspects of yourself.

There, in the old thinking, feelings and belief systems, you need to find your limitation and loosen it, allowing yourself to come forward and experience all of who you are, and realize the gift to the world you have within and for yourself.

You are that gift, to the world, to God, and most assuredly to your own Divine Christ-Self.

CHAPTER II

The Time of Awakening

You must fully understand the responsibility that rests with you at this juncture of human evolution. It behooves you to look closely at what really speaks as truth, that with which your heart resonates and you alone can accept for yourself moment by moment. Now is the time when all that you have imagined can be realized, for everything is of the Creator and Universal Oneness with unlimited potential. You are the creator of your own reality and what it is you choose to manifest or experience as your story.

What is your passion and love that will carry you into new places, enlightening your life to pure joy and happiness of being?

As you continue to practice the finer art of manifestation, you will soon realize how powerful you are when you approach a decision or when it is necessary to bring forth an urgent need in your life. In time, you will only need to sit with the desire in your sacred heart center and apply your intent coupled with the power of your feelings and thought, then proceed with the decision or conscious choice. You will not be led astray, and you will become ever more powerful in the acceptance of who you are and what you choose to create.

Set your intention daily to release control and allow Spirit to guide you as to what is most important. It will be done without stress and done well, for it has already been resolved by your own sub-conscious before you became consciously aware of it in that moment. Thus, creation is not a strenuous act when you allow it to be handled in Divine Timing and in Divine Right Order.

Remain centered in your heart and drop into the space of peace, love, and light and know God is forever here to guide you. He will take your hand and lead you closer to His Being when you seem to fall or are ridiculed, judged or whenever negativity comes to you. Always remember, dear ones, we have walked many lifetimes together since our spark of Light came forth from God. It has all been part of the divine assignment we came in with. We must adhere to our calling and stand in full stature of our Christ Selves, knowing we are never alone. God is by our side, leading and directing us to our greatest achievements.

It is of the utmost importance not to be inundated by thoughts that are not of your own unique belief systems. Many have accepted the beliefs given to us by our parents, educational systems, religious organizations, and society, none of which bear truth of our soul's evolution or speak to the truth of who we are. Thus, it is imperative at this time to be most diligent and pay attention to that which is totally your own belief system, not being influenced by any- thing but that which rings true to your own core being!

There are those who would seek to persuade us from the truth of our path and offer many distractions from our connection with God. Thus, we must monitor our every thought and every word. Our prayers must be of our own making. We are here to further our own individual sovereignty of self, to co-create with Prime Source the new paradigm of Earth in higher vibrations of existence.

Thus, in answer to our prayers and choices, the gifts of God are given at this time to elevate our being to this new energy of creation. The benevolence of God is to gift His beloved children with the opportunity to those who so elect to traverse into unknown territories. None who are seekers of truth shall be left behind or forgotten. We shall enter a unique and beautiful age of such profound enlightenment advancing to the highest vibration of our soul to the highest degree of life, embodying that of the Christ-Consciousness. A Golden Age of peace will exist for a thousand years, or more, should the collective consciousness so choose.

We are urged to let go of everything we believed ourselves, to be opening our conscious awareness to other possibilities and potentialities in the new NOW of existence. It is a period of history when we will come to total self- realization and total awareness of our soul's essence and its pure connection with God. We now need to look at our own core being as to who and what we believe ourselves to be.

Very few people are really living their lives to the fullest extent; they are steeped, instead, in tribal consciousness, doing what everyone else does. What else of life, what else?

There are many with nothing but a static manner of living who continues to play their role with no substance. How long can our people live this way?

Too many are not accomplishing anything, but just letting life go by with no hope for their future. How sad that we have attained this level of non-participation, looking upon life as just the same old thing every day, fraught with redundant, non-thinking work, spectator sports, materialism, non-commitment, and boring repetitive endorsements by a society that aimlessly seeks and searches for listlessness and non-being.

The events of September 11, 2001, changed all that because many are becoming aware and recognizing they are not living their lives to the full- est. Many are now hearkening to the call of Spirit and doing something to reshape, rethink, and re-create their lives, knowing there is much more to be experienced. They are seeking to find the meaning that can catapult them forward into new arenas of existence.

Many will come to realize that their thoughts through their feelings are a governing force that can mislead them. It is, indeed, thought that transforms and beautifies, as well as punishes, judges, and causes much strife and harm on our planet. This negative effect of thought is not necessary for, in God's world, all is of great splendor and magnificence.

God's Love for each of His children reaches into all realms. Know that, as you think and feel, so shall you be!

There is not an Earth-bound soul who does not experience the great changes taking place both on an internal and external level. Those who resist the most will have the most difficulty, while those who understand the dynamics within themselves and remain in faith and trust will find themselves free and unencumbered, surrounded by the Light of the Christ. The window is small for the choice to be made—whether to enter into the Light of a new era of Freedom or remain in the old energies of violence, anger, fear, control, and manipulation.

What will your choice be? Will you move forward into pure Spirit and Love in response to God's invitation as He so provides for His children? We are all God's sons and daughters. Let us come home once again to be with Him in life and in the wholeness of All That Is.

The center of your soul resides eternally within the Seed of God and His abiding love for you, His God-child. So it is, was, and always shall be, on Earth as it is in Heaven. These very words speak to what is now being created on the doorstep of your soul. Heaven on Earth will be the new modality of living life in the full Glory of God and in the Oneness of all things.

As the coming changes take place, it will sometimes be necessary for us, individually or collectively, to move to a new location without any warning. It is imperative to develop the inner guidance to know when such a move is appropriate, to recognize the message when received, and take the necessary action to remove oneself from harm's way.

As Earth begins to move into her new orbit and the darkness comes, people will become fearful and not know what to expect. Remain steadfast in your faith and let the Love of God guide you as to what is the best solution at the moment. The more you can maintain an undivided attention to exactly what is in front of you and pay attention to your inner feelings and intuition, the more you will be able to create for yourself a safe and secure environment regardless of where you are or what is happening around you. By asking for the Christ Light to surround and protect you through all circumstances and by sending this Great Love of the Christ into areas that call for assistance, you are dissipating the negative energy around the situation or people.

When you enact the Divine Law and ask for support from the Great I AM THAT I AM, you evoke the greatest Universal Law, one that cannot be circumvented in any way. It is the most powerful force available to your soul.

As you come to an understanding of this aspect your of Christ-Self, the Great I AM THAT I AM, you will realize you are evoking the Oneness of your Soul in unison with God. He will be in joyful applause for you and those who recognize this greater aspect of Self, for this is part of the Great Awakening. This aspect of the Soul will provide answers in each moment of your daily life.

Much travesty exists on the planet now, and our civilization is feeling it at a deep core level. Thus, our embodiments are reacting with stress, anxiety, and feelings of sorrow and sadness. This is not unwarranted. The new energy is extremely intense. We must remain very focused, moment-by-moment on the task at hand before us especially so when driving, be very present while driving and let the others pass by you blessing them on their journey.

Do not allow your thoughts to wander! We are on information overload, and our minds and brains cannot formulate how to process all the information at once.

Our empathic rate is incredibly high also, thus we have very deep feelings for others and ourselves and what is going on in every area of our life and that of the world. We must remain centered and protect ourselves from taking on negative energy. Especially, through television violence and subliminal messages we receive constantly without our being aware of it.

Realize that God is aware of all of this needless suffering. God is very close to each of us now in the process of our awakening. God will not allow life on Earth to be annihilated. Yes, there will be many departures, but this too is in Divine Hands for no one departs before their time, and it is the soul's choice to do so when ready.

All of us have chosen this time of great change to incarnate on planet Earth. We must honor our soul choices on this journey. Each of us is well aware of these changes on some deep level, although not without fear that some have become totally beside themselves while releasing the old energies and bringing in the new. Thus, we must remain in our closeness with God and in belief and trust of our own Divinity.

As we become stronger in our reliance in our Creator, we will begin to understand things that were neither available nor apparent to us before. We will all eventually come to realize what is true on a very deep spiritual level. Our communication will become ever more important and more universal. We will pause and realize that we have missed a deep connection with each other all these many lifetimes. And we will rejoice that we are communicating that connection now.

We will experience many more beautiful things happening on the planet and many miracles as well. Watch for the miracles, and you will see such as you have never seen before. It is in the spontaneity of the moment that the magic and miracles happen! The true essence of Reality.

Legions of Angels are here, supporting us more than ever. All of the Angelic Realms, including all the Archangels, Ascended Masters, and Great Teachers are present. Assisting humanity as we go through this great change. Remember they are always with us even if we are unaware of their presence. We are their beloved counterparts on Earth. Archangel Gabriel, Archangel Michael, Archangel Raphael, Archangel Uriel, Archangel Aerial et al; All of the Highest Order and are a gift from our Creator to be in service to us. Ascended Master, Jesus, The Divine Mother Mary, all of Jesus Disciples both the men and women; St. Germaine, Buddha, Krishna. All are called now. All are here in the exquisite NOW! These wonderful Beings are gifts from God! As we become ever more aware of the Angelic Realms and that of the Ascended Master Realms, we will actually feel their magnificent presence in full recognition of their service rendered to mankind. We may ask these Divine Beings for assistance in whatever circumstances we feel require their assistance.

Once acquainted with your own personal Guardian Angels and guides, you will find them instrumental in overseeing you Twenty-Four /Seven. Speak to them often and let them become your friends. Guardian Angels are as- signed to us through our entire lifetime, from before we are birthed into this lifetime until we depart. We are assigned one or more Guardian Angel depending on your life's purpose. By acknowledging and accepting their presence in our lives, they too have a "job" to fulfill their divine assignment in the afterlife. Sometimes your guardian angels assigned to you may be a former relative; for instance a father, mother, sibling, or close friend. Someone known to you whom has requested this role and trained for it. I have found all of the angels, and Archangels have a wonderful sense of humor. It is always surprising how and when things occur or show up; unexpected things seemingly occur out of the blue! What fun they have with us!! The adage "where three or more are gathered" is very true and does not mean just three on our side. Our prayers are heard and answered. They also receive our blessings when we send them our love and gratitude. This loving energy is received and supports them energetically with the immensity of the work they do for Earth and all mankind. They are all very grateful for our appreciation of them as they work with us.

We, too, are Magnificent Beings. When we begin to understand and use our own Divine Power, our need for the intervention of the angelic realms will decrease. Through their guidance and efforts in our behalf much is accomplished.

They cannot actually do the work for us, for that would be rescuing, which is not allowed by Divine Law. Therefore, we must look at ourselves to realize each situation, how it was created and how it is to be rectified. And as we do, the Angels will stand by to guide us through the process, nudging or directing as the case may be, but never interfering.

Our life on the planet is of free will and choice, and it will remain so. As free spirits of the Universe, we are all adept at discovering the best for ourselves and how to rely ever more on our intuition and the inner guidance of Spirit to determine Divine Right Action. So we are urged at this time to recognize our highest good and divine right, taking it unto ourselves to incorporate this into our being—our very core being—making it our own.

The gift now is the awakening for those who choose to lift themselves in pure spirit and complete acknowledgement of the Oneness of all. The time has come, the portals are opening! The windows of change are here if you would believe in yourself and your Creator, accepting that which is offered as the greatest opportunity for spiritual growth that humanity has ever borne witness to. The opportunity is to be that of the Living Christ, to embody Christ-Consciousness as Master Jesus stated "this to you shall do and more" bringing forth unto the world "the peace that surpasses understanding."

Come this day and seek your Divine Self. Open to your own inner source of power and creation to the love of your God-self in all its forms. When you look at yourself, whom do you see: self or God? Remember you are of God, made in His image and likeness, pure spirit. Know you are His beloved God- Child!

You no longer need to stand in criticism or judgment of self. When you judge yourself, you are in essence judging God, your Creator. No longer will the old stereotypes of human nature exist for all will be changed and renewed. It is scary to let go of who you believe yourself to be. But ask yourself: From where does my identity come?

These questions are asked over and over these days: Who are you? Are you a manifestation of tribal beliefs instilled for generations? Are you the product of conditioning regarding who and what you *should* be? Or are you, quite simply, God's child, a spark of pure Spirit, an instrument of His Grand Design?

We are all expanding our awareness and actually empowering ourselves, coming forward at warp speed with the changes on our planet. Much excitement exists at this time as we co-create with our Source, both collectively and individually, what we have wanted and desired for thousands of years. Our planet will become radiantly beautiful as she also expands her own awareness into her higher Soul.

A deep love will become increasingly available to all of us who open our hearts and follow our passion and dreams. We will come to the full awareness of who we are. We will know in our Holy hearts, beyond a shadow of a doubt, that we are the perfect children of God created, in every aspect, in His image and likeness.

The majority of people will be reluctant to let go of what they have believed for so long, yet, in time, all will come to know themselves as God's beloved children. All will realize how precious Earth, Gaia, is and that she must be honored and taken care of in the most powerful way possible, for all creation is of the One Life, of God.

Needless to say there is much to be done, for this is a time of much change and chaos as the planet shifts. That is why our choice is so critical at this time. There will be much drama and fear, yet each person in the drama will write their own script and will experience only that which they have, of their own accord, desired or chosen to experience.

This is why it is so important to understand the illusion in which we live and participate. Prime Creator's desire is for His beloved children to be free from the bondage of illusion and to live our lives in total freedom in the new vibration of the human embodiment. Life will change into the likeness of which none have witnessed before anywhere for a new Grand Design is coming forth.

Let us behold the loving God Energy available to us now. How extraordinary it is to have this energy within our being now, to actually know it is of God and His great Love for us. As we incorporate this Love into every cell of our bodies, we become one with it and can hold it ever closer to the Truth of who we are. There is no language to really describe the absorption of such a state of awareness and love. We will know in our sacred heart it is our pro- found privilege to carry this energy of the Christ, to be the instrument of thy Father's goodwill for ourselves and for all humankind. We are blessed above and beyond any and all expectations!

Dear ones, it is from your heart and soul that you must now come to live your life more fully on every level, to experience this profound time of co-creation, to come forward now into the Light and redeem the greater part

of yourself, opening your heart to receive His love for you. Such is the Grand Design of God for you. Extend your hand to the Father this day and come unto His House that you shall be so blessed.

There is a life far greater than we had ever imagined which remains as an untapped reservoir of great potential. It is with great urgency, we tap into that reservoir NOW, to create ANEW. We must come unto the Father's House in the sweet innocence of little children. There is but one House with many ways to reach it. What shall be the way you come unto the Father's House? What is the path you so desire to walk upon?

As it is given to you, as you choose and believe, what then is your choice at this time when all must be made anew? I ask this question as the planetary movement we are experiencing becomes so enormous that it propels us into other dimensions. We are being elevated to that new level both as a planet and within our own conscious awareness. How extraordinary is God's Gift, enabling us to move with Earth into new dimensions of living—and Being.

As people drop the fear and rhetoric they have lived by for millennia, they will have a clearer understanding of what is proposed for Earth and those who reside upon her as beings of Light. We can reach the same awareness in this instant, right now. Regardless of when, change will happen, for all tomorrows are of the present moment and all is created by God and His Great Plan for us at this time.

It is so urgent now on this planet that we radically and vastly shift the vibration so that we may reach this higher level more quickly than expected as the beloved sons and daughters of the Father-Mother God. Thus, we are called to activate the love within our own heart and soul that we may shine the Light of our being enormously now into all aspects of our humanness, expanding this Light energy to all galaxies.

The practice time is over in this drama, and the illusion will no longer have its hold on us. Much has been relayed as to the necessary forces at work in this enlightened time of the Christ Consciousness.

Likewise, dark forces, especially those in control of seemingly powerful places, have propagated much to cause turmoil and fear amidst God's children in an attempt to impede the progress for this great change. It is now time--- and necessary---that we come to a loving state of grace where all is of the One recognizing all beings are interconnected and free.

When the masses have achieved this heightened level of Love, it will far exceed any and all understanding that has ever obtained in any civilization. This Love will represent the highest vibratory rate of existence possible; it will be the creation of Heavenly Earth. Thus, I invite you now to open your Sacred Heart and soul to that enormous aspect of yourself that is all of who you are!

This is an amazing time on our planet, yet also a time of much chaos and turmoil because the old energies are being consumed as the new energies come through. Due to this there is much chaos because there is nothing to keep the old paradigm in place. Life is rapidly changing, and people are becoming more aware that their consciousness is creating the changes; that is why it is so important that we realize how we affect everything by our collective consciousness as well as individual consciousness. Much havoc is created when we do not pay attention to this fact.

So we must embrace the Light and Power of the Divine Intelligence (God) to hold that energy and carry it forward that others might follow the leader, so to speak. Once the few have accepted God's Gift for us, then the masses will follow, as is the law of multiplication or the hundredth monkey effect.

Everything on the planet has been repeated many, many times before as civilization has peaked or reached a plateau. The portrait is not so much different this time, although it is possible to change the outcome if we really understand how important our choices are to all of the galaxies. We are already designing the pattern as we hold the consciousness of the desired outcome. Thus, we are encouraged to come to full agreement of God's Love we so desire and so want to have come forth on the planet.

Life as we know it is about to change drastically; thus, we will be forced to decide what we want as individuals and as a whole. Many have come and accepted a life body at this time just for the express purpose of experiencing this great cataclysmic shift. Many others have come at this time in order to advance more quickly to a higher spiritual level of awareness.

Our Creator urges us to come together now and join in the heart center that the planet may evolve more easily and we may have a gentler ride with the expansion of her Soul.

We are being watched by the planets and galaxy to see what we, as a civilization, decide to do. Our choice is of major importance to the entire universe as this affects the entire cosmos in raising the vibration to that of Christ-Consciousness. All is of the Oneness of our Creator, all is connected from a blade of grass to the entire Cosmic Universe, and thus all are affected in regard to how far we go.

What an honor our Creator has given to us at this time that we are so empowered to have a choice in humanity's evolution. There need be no cause for alarm as God is in charge. So we arrive at this moment in Christ Conscious- ness when we come face to face with all that we are, where we must decide by our free will what our choices shall be!

The more that we give credence to our God Source within, the more it permeates our every cell, every thought and feeling, our every word every moment until we have no feeling of separation from our Creator. This fullness of being does not involve ego or control or any of the dogma so instilled in us today. We are far too powerful as humans in our own sovereignty to continue giving away our power to external sources by projecting outward, rather than holding to the Truth of our divinity within our soul.

Let us come together in Spirit and unite ourselves in honor of God, Prime Creator, and His great Love of us. Come now as children and gather in His Heart this day that He leads us onto the path of perfection and truth, to a new way of being that honors the human spirit and embodiment. Let us create a new design for living on Earth.

As these words speak deeply into your Sacred Heart you may find that part of yourself that has forgotten you are of God. It is not of the intellect or the mental aspect that I speak; it is of your Sacred Heart through which you create the essence of the Creative Power. It is the stronghold of your very Soul's essence and life force. Through this place, you hear the voice of God.

As the loving energy of the people arises on the planet, we will all come to a clearer understanding of God's Plan to provide for His children in The Golden Age. We will reside in the vibration of peace without interference from negative energies. It is imperative that we clear all the baggage we are holding onto in order to reach the higher vibration of this Christ Conscious- ness.

Our existence in this Third Dimensional Illusion is to search for the truth within ourselves. As co-creators with God, we can choose to move forward into this rare opportunity afforded to us or we can remain steadfast in our old thought patterns and beliefs as our identity, blaming God or some outside influence rather than coming to the full understanding that we create our own reality for ourselves. As we experience this change in human consciousness, we are being given an opportunity to lift the veils that have been instilled for so long; we, who are largely unacquainted with our greatness, are now being given the opportunity to open our hearts and to live in the space of our Divinity for we are instruments for change through the essence of the Divine Creative Power.

Awaken, Masters, to your glory and magnificence! We are an indestructible force of light and wisdom now being called forth to assist in the greatest drama ever to behold on Earth. Let us not tarry along the way. We must awaken to all who we are and allow our hearts to open unconditionally to the higher essence of our God-Self, the all-encompassing part of Self that has remained Holy and Sacred throughout all creation. We are invited to join the many who have sojourned into the full realization of their own divinity, coming to the level of Christ Consciousness of Jesus who was so blessed by the Father.

Oh, my beloveds, not until now have we been able to experience our full ability of rising to the highest state of Christ Consciousness as that which Jesus and the many Ascended Masters have accomplished. This is the greatest time on planet Earth when all the good that was promised will come to pass. "The lion shall lay down with the lamb." So it was decreed, and so it shall ever be!

Prayer of Release

*Now is the time of great cleansing and awakening to what is really the
Love of God. Who knows what our future will be? Can you see and feel
all the changes about us?*

*Come now and allow yourself to go inside and be with the Spirit of Self.
Come unto the Father for the door is open as He extends His hand and
heart unto you who are willing to come in the pureness of Spirit to
manifest the Glory of God.*

*Take a minute to rest this day and release all that no longer serves you.
Come to rest in peace at thy Father's feet. Lay your burdens down by the
stream of life and know He is there for you always and forever. Come
play in the Garden of God and know that all despair is transmuted now
as you find the peace that dwells within.*

Amen

CHAPTER III

Evolution, Free Will, and Choice

This Earth world, in the third dimensional reality, was created many millennia ago to give life forms the opportunity to experience existence in a human body. Thus, it was conceived that we would enter into an Earth body and live for a short time to experience the illusionary drama we had designed beyond the veil that separates us from reality and truth. This we did so successfully that we became quite adept at it; in fact, the illusion became a main focus on the planet and allowed a stronghold to take place through which other beings were able to control us—with our permission. We gave our power away to these entities and relinquished all consciousness of our origin. Thus, we created a veil to keep us from remembering our true nature, our origin, which is Love and our reason for being here in a human body on Earth.

This human experience was to be for a short time. However, time lapsed and we became ever more involved in this illusion. The illusion became too dense, and we became like a spider captured in the web of our own conscious- ness, the web of illusion. This gave way to a means of vulnerability, further control, and memory lapse as we forfeited that part of ourselves known as our twelve original strands of DNA. This we did willingly, evolving with only two strands today, which has prevented expansion into our full nature as allowed on the third dimensional plane.

We gave up this power and genetic capability intentionally to see how

we could best operate with less capacity. However, the experiment became too intense and continued for such a long time that we were unable to recapture what we forfeited. Our consciousness became so dense that we began to believe in a limited capability as being all that we possess. Evolution took a dramatic turn at this point and almost succeeded in going backward to a time when we carried but one strand of DNA and were of a very low life form.

Fortunately, our forebears saw the danger of further devolution and utilized that event to propel our species forward and, thus, Homo Sapiens developed into the two-legged species that we are today.

In evolution, as we know, all changes accommodate a period of time in existence, and the body, being an instrument of atoms, protons, and neutrons, changed rapidly. In this process, we became very tribal, mostly for survival, and followed along according to tribal dictates. This means of survival worked very well for many centuries. Although evolvement came slowly, we grew in conscious awareness, became more intelligent, and, eventually, began to use this intelligence to dominate our evolution on Earth.

Originally, we respected and treasured nature as the basis for survival.

However, as evolution proceeded, more of creation was sensed and developed to accommodate life in its new form and being. With the use of the intellect, we could now create all sorts of things deemed possible or important for survival, for example, a wheel, a knife, or a pitchfork. Eventually, with the advent of the computer, the consciousness leading up to the previous generation dissipated and the old energy was no longer of the same form of that which

is coming forth now! This new consciousness, or energy, is of the Christ

Consciousness, of Love, and is of a light frequency expressed through our electronic cellular structure, emotions and thoughts.

As we become ever more aware of this energy and realize that our DNA is capable of decoding light messages, we will experience every-day occurrences that were previously deemed impossible. Certain occurrences will no longer be perceived as miracles but rather as actualities, new ways of creating

with planet Earth that will afford much change for both her and for us as beings of light energy.

We are the instruments who will bring about rapid changes as we enter the Fourth and Fifth Dimensions. This new Creator energy is fully present, causing everything to intensify and forcing the release of antiquated thought forms, systems, emotions and everything and anything that no longer serves our planet or us. It will be like a treadmill, fast paced and rapidly moving. We will sometimes not know if we are going forward or backward as we move into this new planetary orbit, entering the black hole of Light energy (Photon Belt), so often spoken of, which will encircle the Earth in its entirety.

This extraordinary flow of the Christed Energy is fully present now. This energy is here for us to call upon and use. Bequeathed by God to everyone and used by Jesus Christ who, in regard to His miracles, spoke, "This, too, you can do … and more." Now is the time of which He spoke. We are now able to absorb this magnificent All Powerful, Loving God Energy into our core soul cells and allow it to flow through us as Spirit, as the benevolent Being—God so intended.

New times are ahead that will be truly phenomenal. Everyone is very aware of all the changes taking place in all areas of life. What is known today as   'The Shift' is upon us moving us into new paradigms. As our worlds begin to change, we will have to come face to face with our own fears and truth. What we have been hiding from, or under, for so many eons of time. We will become more accepting of the New Age, as it is called even though, after all, information from ancient ages is coming forward again now.

Humanity will no longer have the illusion of strongholds it has cherished for over these thousands of years and will be challenged by things never be- fore experienced. Yet, somewhere in our deepest memory is the remembrance of our Soul-Self (Oversoul), which knows what is true and operable on this planet now. In our core being, we know what to let go of and what will work in its place: new technologies, new means of communication through telepathy, which is merely advancement in our human aspect of God Self, and new energies of all types.

These changes and discoveries are not for us to fear but to glory in. It is an exciting time for all who have waited for this to transpire. At last, our plan- et will place us parallel with sentient beings on other planetary systems who are awaiting our advancement. This extraordinary event is not of our planet alone. Our planet, galaxy, and all Universes will be affected by this great Shift in movement and our raising of consciousness throughout the Solar System.

Fear-based consciousness is all that is withholding our movement (Ascension) and advancement. It has been this way for millennia. Fear has been a means of manipulation and control by our governments, religions, media and many others including the newest, being technology. We also self-create fear from our own consciousness. When humanity removes fear from our consciousness and belief, we will escalate rapid manifestation and movement on the planet. All that has ever been deemed possible in this lifetime will be experienced.

At this transitional time, we have nothing to hold onto or grasp, so we are in a free fall, so to speak. Fortunately, though, as we fall, we are reaching out and we will be caught by Universal energies in the form of new creations of thought. All difficult and demanding things we have incorporated into our

lives on Earth will no longer exist. We will find life to be far simpler and much more satisfying and fun when we are aware of our identity and what is possible to accomplish, as we come to live who we truly are.

These discoveries and our new world will astound and amaze us. They will also enlighten us into a new paradigm of creation.

God's Divine Plan for us and the entire Universe is *real*. It is an invitation to advance His entire universe to a higher level of planetary evolution. Our choice is how far humanity will advance, and it is of major importance. Do we want to fly with the eagles or remain strapped to our Third Dimensional Illusion? This is an option that we all have at the present time, knowing we have free will and choice as bequeathed by God.

Thus, we are challenged with the greatest pivotal time in the history of our planet—whether or not to move into the Light of this new paradigm where we will be sovereign and free in Spirit. Many do not wish to experience this change in the human body and will choose to leave, which is their perfectly right decision. Others will decide to remain here on the planet in order to assist those who also decided to remain. Those desiring to ascend into the Fourth Dimension will do so traveling by light, sound, and thought.

God resides within. Our Creator is a benevolent, loving, non-judgmental Being. He is the Divine Intelligence of the Universe. He awaits our choices and heeds our travel as we journey with our beloved planet into new realms of existence.

Consider the magnificence of all Creation. Consider the beauty and joy of it! God, the Great I AM THAT I AM! God, our Creator, totally aware and totally present within our being. Through God, we will experience all that we decide to experience this lifetime. All that we have chosen to have, do, or be! How grand is that?

All choice stems from the potential in any given moment, which is why living in the NOW (No Other Way) is of imperative importance as we speed ever so forward, swinging between two worlds. It will become ever more important to remain in the present moment, the NOW, where the potential of all creation exists, from where all is coming forth and existence itself began. This new energy is where all things are possible.

The new dawn will be a great time of instant manifestation, instant truths, and wonders beyond our present comprehension. We have nothing to com- pare it to, so our brain cannot store this change in the data banks nor give it any relevance. Thus, for many, even if something is seen with their own eyes, they won't believe it because they cannot relate the experience to anything known.

So what is your choice at this pivotal time on planet Earth? Spirituality, your choices are of paramount importance for your own journey and safe- keeping—and for the journey of all souls.

This is the choice factor and free will that Prime Source instituted as Divine Law.

So what will your choice be? Choose well, my beloveds. Choose well! Those who are open to receive God's love and are desirous of their Ascension will be surrounded by the Light of the Christ and will experience the Christ Consciousness (God). Light, so radiantly beautiful, so pure and full of our Creator's Being that the evolution of the souls, who choose to evolve, will move in quantum leaps into this new dimension.

Your soul part carries great wisdom, not only of the Earth school but all other schools on many different levels and planets. Thus, the journey of the soul penetrates all of your being and guides you to act or react in circumstances that pertain to you, your calling, your level of experience, and your expansion. Thereby, when comes the time that the soul is to journey homeward, it does so by the choice of that particular soul. It matters not what the choice

is, nor how experienced, for the soul in Divine Law or Cosmic Law must be honored for whatever choice it makes.

Those who are open to receive God's Love and are desirous of forward movement of their souls will be surrounded by the Light of the Christ and will experience the new energy. They will experience the new consciousness when the light will be so pure and so full of the essence of our Creator's Being that the evolution of souls will move in quantum leaps to another level of awareness.

The third dimensional reality, as we know it, will no longer be a part of our existence but, rather, a memory stored somewhere in the cellular level of what once was. Is it rapture, you ask, or abandonment of another? Not so, for the Father would never abandon His children. He loves His children, but He will offer each the opportunity of choice as to what it desires to experience at this juncture upon Earth.

We must recognize we are all connected to all life. As we continue to be beleaguered with the strife of one another, the consciousness of one man against another, the belittling of one's self and another, and the continuation of one nation against another, we find ourselves, throughout history, repeating and repeating that which destroys. In truth, we are equals! We are all God's children! We are here to experience life in His Perfection, to love the divinity of the soul! That is life as it will be manifest on Earth henceforth! No longer allowed will be the devastation of our lands and the belligerence of one nation against another or one man against another!

Thy Father's House has withstood much in His Name in all that is Holy.

Too much has been precipitated in the name of religion and control of the masses! Much has been imbued into the soul of each person who walks today in human form that is untrue according to God's Plan that was never true, and never meant to be! Thus it was that humanity was so misled by those whose words were drawn not in the *Love* of God but in the *domination* of God! It was our own folly to believe all that was presented to us!

Now the truth is revealed and unraveled. Now we stand—brother facing brother, woman facing woman, and child facing child—in the full conscious- ness of one another and a planet in jeopardy of destruction.

Now we come face to face with our Creator. What will your truth be? What will your choice be? What is your belief? What are you willing to let go? What are you able to bring forth from the essence of your soul in its darkest hours to rejoice in the Presence of the Lord Christ?

Beloved ones, the hour is soon coming when you will be challenged as you have never been challenged before! It will be your choice, your core belief, that will bring you to the full realization of your God essence, His love for you, His opening of the door so that you might enter. Will you run and hide? Will you choose to keep the door shut and remain in darkness? Or will you accept the truth of the moment, the truth unveiled, and step into the greatness   of who you are!

God is and always will be! Allow your soul to come forth at this time of great change. Choose to walk in the Light of the Christ forever!

CHAPTER IV

Ushering in the Golden Age

In this time of personal contemplation and discovery of ones self, it is vital to allow our negativity or personal issues to come forth on a deep core level in order for the soul to be free of all that encumbers it to move into the new Energy. It is time to eliminate what no longer serves us, that which is deeply rooted on a family, genetic, tribal and spiritual level. We have been of mass consciousness for so long that we are unable to recognize ourselves our own true self as sovereign beings. Many of us have hidden under the umbrellas of all that has been given as a belief. That is why there is much work to be done   and much to be released by the masses. As each of us, as individuals and collectively, change our understanding of ourselves and each other, we provide a   space to affect change in other people's conscious-awareness as well.

Without a change in mass consciousness, the loss of human life will be enormous and it will cause the Earth and other galaxies many problems in the evolution of the Cosmos. The masses no longer can afford to hold on to that which is not true. We find ourselves with a stronghold on fear that incapacitates many of us to move into any other possibilities or potentials that are for the betterment of both individuals and mankind. Fear is causing much of the chaos on our planet. Those who consider themselves to be the owners or gods of our planet at this time are deceiving themselves as well as others. Much unnecessary wrath and destruction is being created for the Earth when in actuality much can be elevated if we care to recognize that it is we who create confusion and destruction with our emotions, thoughts, and actions. The more negativity and fear that is carried forward, the more it is that has to be experienced in learning what is not of truth. Fear must be released to allow for the light to shine through and the negativity to be dissipated forever. A new world is beginning to come through each consciousness as each human consciousness/mind brings forth The Golden Age. The age of pure LOVE that is Gods highest manifestation for His Children. They are not owners of the planet, for no one can own the planet, it belongs to God! They are false gods, humans or other beings attempting to control others through manipulation and fear.

Remember, Earth is a free-will zone of duality. Both light and dark are operating at this time on our planet, and that is causing much of the chaos. We find ourselves with a stronghold on fear that immobilizes many of us from moving forward into potentialities for the advancement of humankind. This is creating much unnecessary wrath and destruction on Earth when, in actuality, much can be alleviated if we choose to recognize that we, through our fear- based thought-forms and emotions, create much of the confusion and destruction. Fear attracts fear. The Law of Attraction is always mirroring us. Thus, you are what you fear. The more fear we create, either for ourselves or society, the more easily we are manipulated and feed that negative energy.

We must release fear to allow our Creator's Love to shine through us. When we replace fear with love, negativity will cease for there is no room in our sacred heart for both to exist at the same time. A new world is emerging as we enter the Age of Aquarius, The Golden Age, the age of pure love made manifest by our Creator. In this new age, we will reach the highest vibration ever gifted to God's children, reaching, as Jesus did, the most Holy Gift to humankind, the gift of Christ Consciousness.

For a short period of time, life will be ever more chaotic, especially in the United States, for through these times of adversity, all of us will learn of our own wisdom, strength, and courage. We are learning how deeply we are connected to one another and every life form. We will learn what is important in living life, what supports life, and what doesn't. We have gone to the extreme in this civilization now, whereby we have ravaged Earth and left her naked. Earth can no longer sustain herself with what we are doing to her. Thus, as we change, so does she. Earth will also become more sustaining for us as we accept that her gifts so misused and abused.

We are becoming more aware of our Earthly home. When we understand the havoc we have caused our Earth Mother including all of the elementals, nature, animals, sea life coupled with the destruction of her waters, lands, air--- wars, mass murder, killing of life in all forms; it affects her total essence of Being! She will become more self-sustaining of the human and other species. We must clean up the mass destruction we are bombarding her with every second, world wide, both physically of her embodiment and with our collective consciousness of negativity. Earth will lose her very life force if we continue in this insanity with no regard of our sacred home and her many precious gifts to us. She knows our every step, and loves us deeply. Earth is a living, breathing planet with a soul. We are as she is, made of her carbon, water, etc. When we no longer put her very existence in peril, offering her our love, both she and nature can become more sustaining to all of us.

During this time of Earth's evolution, not all areas of the planet will be safe or livable. As our Earth changes her biospheres, some of the more toxic areas created by mankind will require much remediation. Negativity that she holds, especially nuclear radiations, must be released in order to detoxify toxic lands and seas. Many of her lands and seas will be uninhabitable for many centuries until her planetary heart and soil are cleansed of our past devastation.

The current fires, floods, earthquakes, and weather changes are all a part of our Great Mother clearing herself of our toxic abuse. This is part of her soul's evolution. We are witnessing today the migration of many species, not only animals and sea life, but humans as well. Many will leave and find special places that serve them as sanctuary. As people migrate, they will be guided and supported by their intuition. There will be little need for much of what is now on the planet that we use to maintain today's artificial lifestyle such as technology, gadgets, fuel, and money. Life will be easier and simpler, and although some will find life to be more difficult, others will find great peace and the ability to live a sweeter life, ever so close to our Earth home and to nature. Much healing is needed in order to obtain this new level of Christ Consciousness on both a planetary level and a personal level for Spirit cannot come fully into our individual or collective consciousness without the pureness of God, the vibration of which would not carry the negativity that is present. Thus, mankind is experiencing much turmoil in order to complete this process, this clearing, this cleansing of all that has been negative for humanity and Earth. The blood shed on the planet by wars and atrocities to humans and Spirit over and over all these many eons of time must cease!

All are at choice point with the opportunity to be a participant in the spiritual evolution to Christ Consciousness and the Golden Age. Fortunately, Spirit is amidst us all and resides within each soul. We will be able to traverse forward on the ray of light and love that is the Christ Energy. The move into enlightenment will become very real to us and very frightening for those who are not already working on their own spirituality. So now is the time to parlay all that holds you back, all that is resistant to you, all that is of both your beliefs and that which speaks of truth to your heart and soul. Trust your ability to learn to love your Divine Self for that is your birthright as a Being of God.

Fear is the great instigator of all that is of the dark. Fear will propel you into places you do not wish to go. Fear is a means to control, and fear has been a mechanism, imposed by those in authority, to lead souls into a stupor for centuries. Now it is time to awaken our consciousness to the Kingdom of God!

During this time of this great shift, Earth will spill her volcanoes, earthquakes will rumble, and there will be great flooding. When the great waters subside, we will find lost cities and remnants of civilizations rising once again on our planet. What we have today will be lost, but much more will come forward to replace it on a grander scale with the continuation of Earth's evolution.

Earth's very nature will be more beautiful than ever experienced for she, as we, will be lighter and brighter. Her colors will vibrate with the light of the sun, and the nights will have a new glow. If you wish, you may be up all night and play with the elementals and fairies, have a conversation with a flower or animals, dance beneath the moon, swing upon the stars, or even fly! More than we could ever imagine awaits us with the unfolding of the Age of the Golden Sun. We will walk again in the Garden of Eden as gifted by our Creator.

Gaia, in her splendor, will become an easier place upon which to dwell and abide. Humanity will also become wiser and gentler, having full under- standing of life. The soul will be in full capacity of knowing and loving the All That Is. Words, as we understand them in our languages today, do not help us comprehend the beauty of Life to unfold these new dimensions. Our choices will be greater than those we have today for there is much to see and learn in the other dimensions in which we will be traveling. We need to rid ourselves of all negativity so as not to be challenged with the same issues that beleaguer us here.

Earth is our training ground where we are learning to make choices that will serve us in all other dimensions. Therefore, be clear about your desires and your requests. Once the unraveling is completed, there will come a time of great grace, silence, and love that will enrapture us and enfold us into this new energy of light. We will feel as if we are very brave souls arriving home after having journeyed far and wide for many lifetimes, seeking and searching.

As humanity gains insight and acceptance into the greater part of itself in this Golden Age, everyone will be a participant, living in the Being-ness of our total Soul-Self, in the Sacredness of the Holy Father, the sacredness of that part of us that is most High. All will experience Being One with God!

The vibrational frequency will be heightened to such a degree that there will be no room for negativity to prevail, no necessity to create that which does not serve our soul's journey or that of any other soul! Hatred, bigotry, fear, wars, and religions—all of these will cease in God's name!

In thy Father's House, all will be encapsulated from whence it came! The Creator's Good is so extensive and expansive that it incorporates everything from a blade of grass to the entire Cosmos.

We are souls who exist everywhere and in all things, not merely on Earth or in a single lifetime but throughout eternity! As we enlarge on all of our possibilities and all potential, life becomes but a mere dream of our own making. In the consciousness of our thought, we create what we are in the drama that we designed before entering this third-dimensional illusion.

We are beckoned now as the beloved children of God to re-enter God's Home and meld within the light and beauty of the Oneness of all things. Our energy as children of God is being asked to come now to trust, accept, and realize that God is in charge, that all is well with us, and that all is well with the Christ in each of our hearts.

This Earthly existence is all an illusion, very deep and unyielding, played in the big theater of life on the third-dimensional level. Our Father-Mother God steps in now and offers His-Her own solution for many millennia of abuse we have perpetrated upon each other and to the Great Mother Ship we reside upon! We are moving into a new age or a new cycle, when man is being asked to either develop his spiritual capabilities or perish. God's Hand is in everything, and it is our Creator's Plan to expand our entire galaxy. That is what is transpiring now.

We have all come here at this time to be of assistance to this movement forward or upward as the case maybe. We give thanks to our Creator for the opportunity at hand to evolve on a soul level to heights our Spirit desires to us to be! We must open ourselves to other truths and to other perspectives of life for we are much more than we seem! We are in the process of ascension for Earth and our civilization. We are co-creating the Golden Age, which has been prophesied for over 2,000 years, "This Earth may pass away… a new Earth will be forthcoming."

The time of promise is close at hand. The time of transition for the planet shall soon come to pass. At this time, many who are fearful of our Creator and do not trust in themselves will choose to leave while others will be challenged to remain and do the work so decreed. The level of energy or vibration will be extraordinary, and major effects will have occurred both within our physical being and our consciousness. In the magnificence of this incredible Gift from God, our soul's choice is to remain in the third dimensional level, cross over, or ascend to the Fourth Dimension and on into the Fifth Dimension of pure Light and Love. Dear reader, there are many dimensions of creation for God is not a stagnant Being but ever expanding our great Cosmos.

What a miraculous adventure we have co-created with Prime Creator at this time! With our expanded consciousness, we are able to have various choices available to all of us for God made this planet a free will zone.

Will you decide to venture forward to the unknown with the many who are making the same choice at this time? Or will you remain with Earth in her third dimensional form while she goes through her own upheavals in order to cleanse all that is leading to her destruction?

Those who remain must be afforded the honor and capabilities to carry out the new Christed Energy on Earth. Difficult though it may be, this is what some have chosen to do in this lifetime in order to attain balance and fortitude, helping everyone eventually be once again integrated in the New Earth, vibrantly alive and beautiful as never before.

Human consciousness, as we know it, will cease, as we become a new creation with full integration of all capabilities in thought and full usage of our spiritual DNA. The embodiment will be fully conscious, radiating energy from the Sacred Heart chakra in an electromagnetic field whereby a level of vibration or frequency will be maintained that uses the full capacity of our spirituality and our enhanced brain capacity.

It is within all of us to readily change our embodiments to a lighter, more highly energized electrical vibration that is operating in an electromagnetic field in harmony with the Earth, which is geomagnetic, thus creating a balance. It is, therefore, of God's Grand Design that our bodies do change in their entirety to incorporate this new vibrational level. There will come a time shortly, when we will come face-to-face with our Creator in order to ultimately understand our magnificence!

At that time, you will receive no support from any other person. For it will be of yourself, by yourself, and that of your Creator! It matters not who you think you are, where you are, what you are doing, nor whom you are with for the change will manifest so quickly and so completely, encompassing each soul on the planet. There will be nothing to do but surrender to that which is upon you.

Those who remain in great fear and who do not trust their Creator and His Love will be the most challenged by this time of great and complete darkness that will surround all things and all life. Some will think it is Armageddon, the end times, and that God is creating havoc with them personally as well as with the planet. Others will know and face this time with their own core belief and knowledge that it's God's way of delivering to us a new consciousness, a new understanding of empowering who we are, gifting us all with complete awareness and fullness of a new way of living life on Earth!

As the hours of darkness approach the planet, many will feel it coming and become panicked and rush about in fear. The Earth will stand still and each being will be surrounded in the darkness or the light, depending on the individual consciousness. At this time, there are issues we will be looking at on a very deep level, the deepest ever on a soul level. The Earth will literally move into another orbit and placement in her pivotal axis. Atlantis and Lemuria will reappear, while other continents will disappear for cleansing.

Those who choose to remain on Earth will be led to sacred places of a higher vibration. Those who are ascended will assist each other in the Fourth Dimension and the Fifth Dimension and beyond. We spend much time in the Fourth Dimension already, unaware to each other that we are in this heightened vibration. When we ascend to the Fifth Dimension, we shall awaken to our being in the same place but at a different frequency and a heightened sense of awareness. Although things will appear to be the same, we will have our full capacity to know who we are.

The great Father-Mother God has deemed it possible at this time to further advance the level of His children's consciousness that we may claim our rightful inheritance on this miraculous planet Earth! This advancement is twofold for not only will Earth be a beautiful specimen of a planet, but humanity will also ascend to a higher level of consciousness, Many souls desire

to be on earth at this time and many are coming in whatever way possible, for this time creates the greatest opportunity for the biggest leap in consciousness ever experienced by any form and in the evolution of mankind.

A world of peace will be made manifest within our own collective consciousness whereby all the dimensions will be made available to us! All the loved ones, Angels, and Masters we so desire to see will be here for us. They will once again walk upon Earth and intermingle and be seen by all of us.

For we will see them and experience them and work with them. We will understand, at Their level, God's intention for us. What a joy and what a Gift of Heaven from God that will be! We will experience the reality for which we have prayed, "On Earth as it is in Heaven." No one will be stuck in this third dimensional framework. No one will be held back by time and space constraints of linear thinking nor controlled by those who would attempt to control the masses. Once we release the fear that this third dimensional illusion seemingly perpetuates, we shall all come to realize the magnificence in The Gift.

Earth is moving to a higher vibrational frequency. She will no longer carry or permit negative energy, pollution of her sphere, or abuse of her waterways, and those who wish to remain on her this lifetime will be supported. Those who honor and protect her, working with her natural ways and means, will be shown how to sustain themselves through all the changes. Those who choose not to live in this abundant atmosphere, to depart, or to live elsewhere, such as planet Earth II, in the process of creation, will be able to do so at this time as well.

We are at a choice point, you see, and singularly it is most important decision any life form has ever made at any time, in any way, and at any moment on this planet. Choose well, my friends. Beings from other worlds are observing us! They want us to progress, and they want to progress further in their own evolutionary process and to interact with the human species so that we may share our love, knowledge, wisdom, and technology.

God is the source of all this change. He wants that we may live in the peaceful manner so desired by humanity. It is of great importance that each of us begins now to evaluate that which is to be our choice and exercise of free will. It will be the most vital decision we have ever or will ever make in this lifetime or in any other.

Imagine, if you will, all Earthly beings living in perfect harmony from the heart and from a state of soul recognition without ego, strife, fear, or anger, without all the negative lifestyles imposed upon mankind by those who are here to be of disservice. Instead, imagine being supported and provided for by listening within and hearing explicate directions on how to live, follow nature, tend crops, care for one self, and birth new creation on this planet. Imagine following your inner guidance at all times and operating at peak performance. This can and will be ours, to live in such a state of complete and pure love, such a Divine State of Being that there is no room for disarray or negativity that has prevailed for so long upon this planet and within other galaxies! How magnificent a Gift God has given to His children that they have this choice, and, yet, how important it is that they choose well.

The entire universe depends on our humility. How could we have been selected as stewards of Earth when one looks at all of our misgivings and pre- mature consciousness about all of life? How could we, as humans, have been given the post to advance in consciousness to such a degree that we affect All That Is, all things everywhere, just by how we handle what is forthcoming?

Beloved Father, you are very brave and knowing to trust in your God Children, to entrust us with such a privilege to expand in consciousness to the extent that all can expand.

Prayer

Beloved Father, you have entrusted us with such an enormous feat at thistime on Earth! Earth Mother, you have entrusted yourself to us so that we can support you in your own conscious evolution. May we carry Earth to her pinnacle now so that she may become the Golden Sun radiating her love to the entire solar system. We, the human race, are the way showers now for all life everywhere. How magnificent that we are so powerful and wonderful in our loving energy, and how humbled we are to think we are created in Your image, in Your light, love, and magnificence!

AMEN

CHAPTER V

Creating Heaven on Earth

This is a time is of great change indeed, but it is also within the confines of creating balance. Therefore, we must remain centered and present as much as possible. This requires the utmost attention to our awareness of what is going on in the world and in our own lives. We must not allow fear to restrain us from living our lives; rather we are to live in the Exalted State of Oneness.

Does this mean we should not live life or retreat to a remote area and hide? Indeed not, for it is a time of development and awareness coming forth, when all of our gifts will become known. Now is the time we have anticipated for so many lifetimes, being in training so to speak, in order to bring forth our knowledge and wisdom.

We will see a renewal of that which was lost so long ago, that which affords us the opportunity to be totally self-sustaining and self-reliant. Thus, there will be little need for outside sources to furnish everything, including the means to live. We will find it's easier to be creative as we bring forth all that is in the highest order of life on the planet, and we will do so with great light and love. We will find areas of love never before anticipated and a quickening of our cellular structure to the point of feeling lighter and ever more compassion- ate. This will allow us to embrace that part of ourselves that has so longed to be recognized.

We will embark on a new level of understanding of creation that far surpasses anything we have been able to previously comprehend at this level of realization. This level of understanding is far superior to anything experienced by any civilization to date and will advance humanity from the confines of limitation. There will be no conjecture left for us to hash over as truth or untruth. We will know, and it will be true of all humans to be in greater understanding of the Universal Principals.

This is the Christ-Consciousness, the divinity of each soul brought forth now, awakening to a higher level of consciousness. Yes, these Universal Principals and this Christ Energy have been there for us to utilize, but we were totally unaware of these Universal Principals or how to access this new energy. We were not at a level in our development where we could accept the reality of these Truths. We are there now! We have set our course with the winds of change that all may live in rhapsody of God's Love for each of His children, a level of consciousness in complete recognition of the Oneness and Perfection of all things. Indeed, our individual uniqueness and the power of our thoughts and feelings to create anew is the greatest gift of God always.

Our soul's purpose is to experience life as the expression of Prime Creator, to expand even further into His Creation and individual projections for us, into a nonlinear, timelessness and non-dimensional reality of existence where all is possible to experience.

Great potentiality exists now for us to live amidst each other in peace, harmony, joy, and love. God's greatest desire is for all to live in peace with no wars or disharmony amidst His offspring? How magnificent is this? How grand that we, by our choice for change, would allow our Creator to expand our awareness of Earth and planets in other galaxies. This is not of a lesser God but of a greater God who has much beauty, joy, and limitless creation to share with us.

Heaven on Earth? Yes, why not? All we have to do is allow, accept, and be open to receive, know, and trust in ourselves and, in the doing, trust in God and His Divine Love for us.

The very words as spoken by Jesus, "We are made in the image and likeness of God" invokes us to a heightened level of our Exalted Self. Let us refrain from dwelling on the past rather seeking the future in all its untold glory. How we can achieve our great Higher Self, our Exalted Self, our Soul Self? Reach now into your core being and feel this potential of   yourself moving through you and desiring to be an instrument of creation, an expression of Divine you. We are the Avatars of light building the build the bridge of the New Tomorrow. This new world awaits our arrival in this expansion of the Christ-Consciousness that is carrying us into ways only dreamed of. Ways of existence only written about or prophesied. It is all there. We just need to believe it and choose it for ourselves, being the light weavers of this new Earth in co-creation with God.

Time is relentless in its control over us with its dominion of our every movement. Suppose there was no time that it stopped and we were set free. Suppose we could move freely about and manifest each thought, each movement or desire. This is the true level of creation, of manifestation, such that we have our Being in any dimension and in whatever way we desire to manifest, through Love.

What of *the zero point* soon to be experienced by all of Earth and her inhabitants, when everything slows down and comes to a stop? What will your reaction be to such phenomenal change of present reality? Will you be able to withstand it and move through it with full awareness of your new Self and your new state of consciousness so that you will only want to experience more of the dynamics of the Creator's new Earth home?

How will you handle this moment when all will be at a standstill and people will be challenged to face themselves to a depth they have never done before? Where will you place your trust? Where will find your love of self?

How will you react in total darkness or light as the case may be within the confines of yourself when you get to see all of whom you are and the many aspects of your being? Will you see only darkness or will you see the Love of your Creator supporting you and carrying you forth through this period of darkness upon the Earth? Will you partake of it as a blessing or a curse, as God's wrath or His Divine Love for us?

What will you do when a total clearing and healing of both your physical being and your soul's essence prevails? Can you go beyond fear? Can you face all you are and all you have ever been?

What of this change upon the Earth? Are you strong enough to withstand her movement of slowing down and revolving in the opposite direction, realizing that you will also be revolving in the opposite direction of polarity?

God will sustain and support you if you trust enough, if you allow His love to penetrate your being and encompass every cell to your core essence. Will you stand in Love of your Christ Self as God or will you whither and tremble in fear, holding on to old belief patterns that no longer serve you?

Always remember the statement: "The Father and I are One." God now extends to His beloved Earth children all Love, Wisdom, and new ways of existence without the beliefs and limitations that have held us back from ourselves for so many, many civilizations. Will this new rise of civilization be the one that circumvents all others and releases us from our ego so that we might choose another way, another belief or truth, a level of awareness never achieved before on this planet Earth so beloved of God?

We have the opportunity to choose to succeed within this new evolutionary process so that we might achieve such heights as never experienced previously anywhere in any galaxy. Can we, as a collective consciousness, achieve the totality of this great movement to the heightened level of Being that God anticipates us to achieve? It is up to each one of us, beloveds. It is what we choose for each other and ourselves in order to reach the pinnacle, the Arc of Success, and the dominion for which we have strived for millennia.

Reach high, dream big, and choose to expand to your highest potential! Swing from a star, gazing at the Earth as she shines her light ever so magnificently amidst the entire universe. It is for us to choose to implement God's Grand Design as He holds fast to His Own

Consciousness for humanity to be all they have ever desired to be. Many are coming forward who can lead and assist with their knowledge and ancient wisdom to a new paradigm, a new enlightened species whereby all live with reverence for themselves and that of the God who resides within.

Nothing else will support the dynamics of this Divine Self other than that of complete faith and trust of our soul connection with our Creator. Many will believe they have succeeded in this stronghold of enlightenment. However, as the actual time of truth occurs for mankind to be revealed to their Maker, how many will falter in their belief.

Now is the time of speculation, the time to go within and contemplate just who you are and how you came to be through all of existence. What are your core beliefs? When you are faced with the Presence of God, what will your reaction be? Will you run in fear as many have done in the past or will you realize the greater part of yourself, joined in this radiance of Oneness and Wholeness?

God cherishes all. He abandons or leaves no one behind. All will have the choice of their free will to follow whatever is of their heart, of what speaks truth to them. It is a critical juncture at this time when we shall be so challenged. So choose well, beloveds that you may live in the Majesty of thy Father's Mansion, Heaven on Earth.

But we also have another choice: that is, to remain in the remnants of third dimension to re-create what we already have experienced, with the possibility of reverting to a time past such as the stone age or worse. It will be a difficult existence on a planet that is beautiful in her simplicity yet unwilling to continue with the pollution and degradation that have wrought her destruction. Does this message of choice bare repeating once again to satisfy those who choose to remain in the dormant state of human evolution and not venture forward to all that God has prepared for His beloved children? Awaken, slumbering children! Harken to the Call!

Some will take this course and some won't. On Earth, being a planet of free will, some will hold steadfast to the old ways. They will find they have that choice and will stay in the planetary cycle or vibration as it remains in a third dimensional plane of warring and needless destruction. Yes, they will be venturing backward rather than forward for Divine Law states, "It is always given to you as you believe," and, by Divine Choice, given to God's children.

Imagine a new world, a place only of pure love and reverence for God and you and all other persons and creatures and life forms, a place so great and pure of love where all is of peace, harmony, and the joy of living! This is the future! This is the design of the New Earth. This is thy Father's Kingdom.

Would you not choose freedom as you have never known, love as you have never experienced, peace that surpasses all understanding, health in all aspects of your being, and movement within dimensions? Has not the prayer been for centuries, "On Earth, as it is in Heaven"? Has that not been the request throughout these many lifetimes? Are we not asking for Heaven on Earth each time we verbalize His prayer? What is Heaven but that of the Father's Kingdom, that of a greater design for His children?

The time has come for His Grand Design to be delivered unto us as requested. It is always given to you as you believe. The deliverance is now of Heaven on Earth. What a beautiful Golden Age awaits us, one of pure love energy whereby the New Earth and her inhabitants are transformed each within the other for Earth, too, is made of the same material as we are.

Therefore, are we not she and she us? Such will be an evolution of mankind as never before accomplished throughout all eternity. All peoples of Earth will be in their finest garments, clothed in their Divine Self and Heritage. Each soul shall choose based upon its belief of its sovereign self.

What will your sovereign soul's choice be? Will you journey forward in full trust of yourself and God's Love for you? Or will you remain intact, as you are, never evolving to the Higher State of God-Consciousness.

Prayer

Dear God, how can we best advance the planet to reach her pinnacle of pure radiance? How can we reach the Golden Age and the thousand years of Peace?

We, as humble human beings, have this extraordinary opportunity to be all that You have anticipated us to be.

We are the gods and co-creators. We are God's children and the instruments for change. We are the bearers of Christ Consciousness, uplifting all life everywhere. We are extraordinary Beings in our human embodiment, forever in search of Truth. Thus, Father, we are who you know us to be, the Gods-Goddesses who walk Earth so that all beings may have a life of lasting peace.

AMEN

CHAPTER VI

A New Way of *Being*

These are challenging times for our planet and for each of us as individuals. May the Psalms comfort us, *"Yea, though I walk through the valley of the shadow of death, I shall fear no evil for thou art with me."* The Father speaks to us, *"Fear not for I am with you from this day forth and forever more. I cometh to you now and rejoice with you in the newness of life, the creation of all things new and in the joy of my Love for you."*

Never would He leave us in our hour of need at this time of great change and upheaval in the process of rebirthing a new planet, a new loving consciousness, a new life of joy, love, and peace. Come now, my beloveds, and let us walk together this day, spend time together in unwrapping some of the misgivings we may have about this time on our planet. Let us explore the

truth brought to us now to ready ourselves in the wisdom and knowledge that all humanity has waited for.

All galaxies and all universes have waited for this time, this great movement forward to new and unparalleled ways of being. Thus, the changes on Earth affect our galaxy, universe, and planets forever! This is no small feat! It is no small one-time event but the most powerful event ever to occur on this planet and in this galaxy and the cosmos! Yes, beloveds, the universe awaits us. Yes, beloveds, the universe is questioning how far along we are and what our choices will be. Its advancement and existence depends very much on what we do for we are all One in the eyes of God. All Creation is made manifest from this one Source. We must choose through our hearts and choose what is true.

It is of the utmost urgency now that we pay attention to every subtle energy we are aware of and heed the call to listen to that still small voice, rendering it more powerful than ever before as the Earth swivels on her axis and we swivel with her. We will be challenged to remain conscious of our spirit and our soul's purpose. We will be challenged more than ever before in any lifetime for it is the dynamic of this lifetime, this rapid acceleration of time speeding up along with the escalation of planetary awareness, of no-time and no-space, this epic in the evolution of all galaxies and universes when we will reach the pinnacle of evolution more so than has ever been accomplished before on Earth.

Are we as a race, humanity, open to move consciously with her in this great progression of Spirit, allowing this evolution to go as far as possible as we ride with Earth, with God in His wanting for us, His children, to be free living in a heightened vibration of existence? It is a way of existence that is totally free and beyond our worldly comprehension at this time, but wholly of God's creation and desire for us to have that which we have wanted for ourselves forever!

In the past, we have prevented this advancement out of fear, control, and all other adversities. We have been shaped by what has been forced upon us for millennia. It is our birthright to have the wonder and beauty of God and all of His gifts bestowed upon us now as a people, and a civilization, endowed with that of the Christ Consciousness of total pure Light and Love.

Come now and listen to these words. Listen to them and feel them. Know they speak to you at a soul level as you recognize the truth in them. Know this as you open to your own divinity and rapid acceleration of growth. You will be astounded as to how powerful you are within your own Being and your own development, no longer relying on the outside, on others, on the government or whatever concoction has been derived to take your power. Rather, you will rely on your very own divine Self, your sovereignty.

There is a powerful you who is forever one with God, one with your own soul-Self, as God. Accept this truth as being of the Father's desire for you and what was imparted to you through Jesus. Accept, finally, you're God- Self and your own part in all of this play enacted so long ago of which we are all back now to correct and change. We will find ourselves in a very precarious position if we continue on this path with the same belief and systems, for they are not sustaining us as a free people of our own self-reliance and sovereignty. From this tyranny we cry freedom, as children of God, to live as we would from our hearts and to love in the manner that was bestowed upon us by our Creator! This is our birthright, and this is our calling now as individuals to accept this birthright, to accept the greater part of Self, to acknowledge that there is more in the universe than the parcel that has been sold to us as a bill of goods by greedy human systems that don't work anymore because they're not serving the people. There is so much more!

Do you believe the Creator of all universes can only create on this plane, this one dimension? As stated, thy Father's House has many mansions. What of those mansions? Where are they? Are they not beyond as well as upon the Earth? Is it not possible to have many existences within the One? Of course it is. Such a mighty Being as God would delight in creating existence within existence within existence. It is not a stagnant God, rather an ever-expanding Creator God. We are now going into this new phase of existence.

As our scientists learn and expand in consciousness, there will be much more discovered? We will be able to reach the height of the Golden Cities and The Golden Age to come? After all, we are enlightened Beings, striving for Perfection within our very soul to the extent that *ALL* is of the Absolute, of God.

Is this not beautiful? As the co-creators with God, we are able to achieve such dynamics in this spectrum, moving into Christ-Conscious, a state of awareness never achieved in human form before or after Jesus, until now?

The backward spiral or the spiraling downward will no longer be necessary and no longer supportive to those who have been in control for so long, those for whom we have, as humanity, given our power away.

Thus, as the darkness ebbs and the light transform's the dark, there will be much chaos, and turmoil with the releasing of old patterns and systems that no longer serve. Much greed, possession, and control has been exerted over all humanity for many, many generations. It must cease now in order for the unfoldment of the planet's evolutionary process to expand and bring in the new rise of civilization.

Many civilizations have been here, and many have gone, but they remain in the ether of existence for all time. Thus, the pinnacle in time has come when everything is changing and releasing like never before. All energy of civilization that has existed on our planet is here now to raise, heal, and release that which did not serve it during its time frame, such that the etheric may be cleared of all negativity.

We have all returned over many, many lifetimes to re-create for ourselves with God in the *new dawning,* the new energy arising in our evolution of man- kind. How far forward we will expand and how extensive the changes will be is dependent upon the human race and its capability of accepting new ways.

 It is dependent on our letting go of the old beliefs and that which is no longer our truth. Thus, we human inhabitants can only go so far if we are en- capsulated in a school of old thought and cannot release this part of ourselves to the universe for healing in order to incorporate the new form of creation using the Christed *Energy* within the new dynamics of manifestation.

It is instant and in the moment that this manifestation is creating itself. Thus, we must be of the highest integrity in all areas of our life. This requires us to be genuine within ourselves, having a constant vigil of our thoughts and feelings given them, holding that vigil of light in all that we do. Choice is par- amount now, as is the awareness and intuition to follow our highest good and let go of anything that holds us back from being wholly who we are. It is time to release that, which does not serve, that which does not allow us to fly free!

Yes, we have instilled many rules, regulations, and ways of being that have been so deeply ingrained within our core that we don't know what real freedom is, nor real truth. The old energies and the old patterns of thought, which we believed were right and true for us, have held us in control. So accepting were we of this power of outside forces that few, throughout history, questioned it. It was, and is, easier to give responsibility to others rather than to accept our own power. Thus, control of humanity was easily accomplished. We were but sheep led down the path of no recourse for so many centuries, becoming ever-smaller thinkers and doubters of our own power. It is the immediate that we tend to focus on rather than the bigger picture of what is truly happening to us as humanity.

Fortunately, there are those who believe in Truth, those who have full consciousness of what is possible as potentialities. What is *real* and what is an illusion. Christ Consciousness is what we are creating now – the full potential of each human being living in total freedom, totally supportive of our human nature. We are capable of living in the fullness of God's energy in the form of Light and Love, that of our Divine Self, without the need for technology and gadgets we utilize today.

A new creation is dawning— new dimensions of love, peace, harmony, and joy. What we need for ourselves is to inhabit our planet in human form without depleting her resources and without adding our negativity to her. We need to create an Earth existence so pure, so full of light, that she shall shine forth though all nature and all levels of reality. Her light will emanate to and through all things, including human beings as Gaia captures and enraptures and holds each of us to her bosom. We are here to nourish each other and our Earth Mother in her full capacity of expansion and in our acknowledgement of her natural gifts of sustenance and well being.

Thus God Speaks: *"Take drink for I am the Source of all life. I AM the Bringer of Life, All That Is, the Bearer of Light and Truth."* Let your light shine, let it radiate forth into all things and all places. You are My co-creators. Raise each soul into the Light of Creation that it may come forth in all its glory and joy of this evolution in recognition of your Creator.

What does a father or a mother feel when their love, so freely given, goes unbeknownst to a child? Or when the child decides for itself through the dictates of a society or tribe that has been misled for so many thousands of years? What does God, our Father, do when He has bequeathed to His sons and daughters a universe of free choice and free will? Is that not the greatest honor any father or mother could ever possibly bequeath to a child, the opportunity to be a free creator of one's own universe of free choice, to experience whatever their soul's desire during any lifetime? Is this not the most profound manifestation of life possible by that of the One who holds us most dear?

Have you been open enough to rethink and question from whence your beliefs come and from whom? Have they been derived from the tribe of which you live? Have they been instilled in you from childhood, from your developing years before and up to seven when you were most influenced by your parents or whoever was significant in your life? How deeply, as children, we are affected, unbeknownst to our young impressionable minds, unbeknownst even to those who love us and are the source of nourishment during those very impressionable years of childhood development.

But what of it now? Why do we carry such things that no longer serve us? Why, to such an extent, do we actually live with what is not even ours, what never was ours, but was given to us as a belief? Why not bring forth a new beginning of creation, a new awareness whereby we are not under the disguise of another, where we are capable of all of our attributes in every facet of our being to be the absolute totality of who we are and what we are all about, our God Self?

We shall hold ever more closely to our Creator recognizing that as the true Source of our Soul on this ancient and beloved planet Earth. We shall claim all that is appropriate and all that is ours now. We shall allow all of our Being-ness to come forward as our Father-Mother God intended.

Yes, that includes the shadow as well as the light. God has granted us the polarity of our soul for its growth and experience of all potential, that we may decide what truth is and what truth is not. Our perception would not be possible if all of us were of the same manifestation. Thus, we are able to learn from this earth school as we grow, experience, and know ourselves ever so deeply.

It is the design of the soul to want to be all that it can be, to experience all that is unlimited in the eyes of God that is His gift. Yet, how many live their lives under the false pretense that they are all they can be? What if we, out of fear of change, miss the greater part of our Being, of our Soul? How often do we decide to accept less, believing it is right to remain in the status quo rather than taking the risk for change? How often do we dare to say, "Yes, God, I am here and I am willing to recognize you as the larger part of who I Am, to do your work, to step forward in your name as One, not separate but together in our greatness and our love for one another?"

No other love has ever been greater, now or ever after, to experience all that thy Father has for His God-child, to *feel* His love penetrating every cell of your being, to fully express that part of yourself who is the totality of creation by expressing and feeling this radiance shining forth from your own Light within. Thus it is done! The abiding grace, the peace that surpasses all understanding! The beauty and joy of knowing there is nothing separate from you and that of your Source!

Your birthright is to take this ownership of your Christ Self and relish in its power and essence and joy, to live from this highest attainment possible when you are joined in total recognition of your soul Self as being that of the Creator God. Thus, we are ever deepening that connection, ever speaking to our own self, our God Self, ever knowing what is true for us at our deepest core level. In this knowing there is absolute faith and trust in our Creator and ourselves.

The premise of separation is no longer valid. Under the illusion of having to give our power away, we are recognizing that all we ever heard or were given as "truth" is no longer valid.

There is no room for illusions in the future for illusions are strictly fictional and only operational by those who wish to manipulate mankind. We willingly chose to allow others to lead us where they would and to take our power away. We did that of our own accord, abdicating our responsibility to God and ourselves.

Nothing was enacted without our consent on some level and at some time. It matters not when the agreement was made. What matters is that now is time to regain our rightful heritage to be free souls, unencumbered by man's folly or control.

But they cannot control our very souls. Today, we are asserting our intention to be free to express what we may, free to walk this Earth as we so desire, free to be ever present to our Source-Creator, free to be one with humanity with our hearts opened wide and baring our souls to express ourselves in our highest potential.

How rapidly one changes! How rapidly things change when God is recognized as good, unlimited resource and unlimited potential every instant, every breath and even before breath itself. What of our connection to Source and His abiding Love for us, we, forever guiltless and sinless in this great Love?

He waits for His Children to realize how great a love He has for them. All life, as He created, is to recognize His great love for humanity that they may step into this Love and absorb this vibration of Love unto themselves.

When will humanity finally stop long enough to feel this, to know this truth, and allow God's Love to flow through its soul? It is tending to one's garden, watching it grow and flourish such that one would never be the same again, nor would one want to be. What seed was planted that now needs germination, addressing and maintaining. So, what of this? What of your soul's desire? What is your soul's desire to feel, to be, to grow?

The old ways served at one time when the times warranted all that transpired, for mankind knew nothing different. Thus it was willed and chosen to have the wars, the battles on all fronts, not allowing the freedom of man to experience that of this great love. Frontiers and boundaries were established amidst each other by humanity, self-inflicted by ego and by prejudices. Many structures came into being unwittingly to the masses and under the guise of much control to keep the mass of humanity from its own beautiful soul Self.

What of this? What is our choice at this critical juncture of change presently felt as an undercurrent by all humanity and all life forms on this earth plane? We are venturing forward, realizing there is much of which we have been unaware, much we have slumbered through, much we have forfeited for many centuries in the name of what we believed to be of greater good. Now our great society begins to crumble and decay from the inside out. We feel the infrastructure topple as we bear witness to Earth's devastation by our very own hands. Now we come face to face with what is real, what is transpiring, and what has been neglected. And what our very core feelings are regarding this illusion that we have constructed for centuries and centuries.

How could we have been led astray so far afield from that of God's greater desire for us? What source would have the ability to persuade us to give up all that we innately held dear to us? The question is posed to you, dear friends, what indeed? Ask yourself this, "Where were you on that fateful day of nine-eleven? What did your soul convey to you as truth when the energy of the people of Earth, as measured by space satellites, surrealistically spiked; or during the change from December 31, 1999, to January 1, 2000, when the people of Earth stood in love unison to welcome the new millennium?" What did your soul bear witness to?

America changed on that day. We lost everything. We have no basis of who we are as a country. Since nine-eleven, rules and regulation. Took away freedoms. No privacy. At that time, an eagle message came across the Inter- net. Tears on the eagles eyes. I wrote the eagle's wings have been clipped.

Indeed, the eagle flies no more because we're not a free country any more. We're giving too much energy and power to those who wanted to create this energy and tyranny. We've robbed our own people. Anything you give energy to grows. Our government had bin-laden and let him go because they needed someone to chase. That's the way our government works. We've even re- moved the word "God" from our nation's symbolism. "One nation under god" is still vital. Many have stood up and died for our country, but no one upholds the truth. …. And that's what we're taking back now; we're taking back our power.

As people come together more and unite unilaterally, they will realize there is no separation that all is of the Divine Oneness of God. This will have a very large impact on humanity and the false belief we have accepted over the centuries. In order to attain a higher level of consciousness and to create a new tomorrow, we must let go of everything of the past and our present situations in life that continue to hold us back.

The human way has always been to make everything historical and to hold on to such an extent that it becomes ingrained within the consciousness, such that one cannot move beyond and let go in order to manifest something greater. Thus, we repeat the experiences. This is true of the Holocaust and the many wars of all centuries, the belief that the only way we can stop something of such a desperate magnitude, such as terrorism, is to remember all that brought us together, to hang tight to every little thing that was ever done to humanity in the past, no matter what its cause. This is a misguided belief and one that has caused many failures of worlds and civilizations that preceded this current one. Mankind must realize it is through conscious thought, along with our emotions, that our reality is formed and created. We are the creators of our own reality, individually and collectively. *As we think so shall we be.*

The more we carry the negative aspect of *what was* and what we *believe* to be true, the less impact the new level of Christ Consciousness will have on our being. Thus, we must no longer search or run amuck to look under every rock and limb to follow many leaders but know within our very souls the truth of what is! We must be in such high want for nothing for we lack nothing for all is of us and around us.

Imagine an existence that is beyond that of the Garden of Eden, beyond that which has ever been; an existence of pure life and dominion over oneself in perfect harmony with creation, one another and the Oneness of all things. This is Perfection! This is offered to us, beloveds, but we must become aware and be selective in choosing that of God's Love. We must choose to love ourselves as the great I AM Presence that we are. We must allow God's Love vibration to be that of who we are, allowing our soul Self to expand in our conscious awareness, knowingness and enlightenment. We must choose to be in the divine flow of life with that of our Earth amidst all that is occurring at this time of the greatest changes our planet has ever experienced.

It is not for us to take everything that happens in this life and carry it with us. Rather, for us to experience and learn, to gain what we can from life and let it go, to forgive those around us who partake in the experiences of life, acting as a catalyst for us to see things differently or to change and move to another level of awareness.

The very act of forgiving ourselves, as well as those around us, is a form of releasing. When we surrender to God that which is, and is not, God assists us in being free from the burden of creating more baggage. This is what life is calling us to do now, to forgive, and to release all of the baggage we have carried forward for so many years. None can be released until all is cleared. No one can be cleared until everyone benefits by the clearing. That is what the planet Earth is striving to do at this time. So too is the human race striving to clear all that does not serve at the present time.

Soon the soul of each person will be in full recognition of the Oneness, not of an ego or a personality, not of others or their interpretation of that soul, but of the whole and completeness of each individual soul and its pure essence.

Everything a soul creates for oneself or experiences is a part of God. God is Omnipresent. There is not a spot where God is not. We need not be afraid or in fear, nor judge ourselves, for God is an allowing and forgiving God. There is no judgment on the part of God; we are the ones who judge and betray, and we are the ones who inflict pain and sorrow!

In thy Father's House are only joy, peace, love, and divine grace! The door is open would you choose to enter! Knock and the door shall be answered! With your divinity the call is being made, asking for permission for the door to be open now! Come, dear ones, let thy Father take thy hand and hold you ever so close to His Heart as you traverse forward to unbeknownst lands. Let His Love for you show the way, leading you to greener pastures!

How could we, as humans, have been given the post to advance in consciousness to such a degree that we affect All That Is, all things everywhere, just by how we handle what is forthcoming?

The Beloved Father is very brave and knowing to trust in His God-children, to entrust us with such a privilege to expand in consciousness to such an extent that all can expand. And how wonderful for us! Here is our opportunity to experience Love of the Highest Order, The Love of the Divine that is of the Christ, a Radiant Love of pure Light energy.

The Beloved has entrusted us with such an enormous feat. Earth has entrusted herself that we support her in our own consciousness. We, the human race, are the way showers of all life everywhere. How magnificent that we are so powerful and wonderful in our loving energy!

And how great is our joyous responsibility! It will be ever more imperative that we get much more rest and allow ourselves time to be alone, to re- main unattached, and to be in nature for nature will relieve the energies from our bodies and lighten our souls.

Know that all is in God's Hands. The great Is-ness of Life. Our mission is to be in service to our fellow man and, in particular, to each other as the light workers join together and ever more closely weave the new dynamics of energy patterns around the planet. It is our design and energy that creates this new webbing that supports the planet and the grid through all things.

Thus, all of us are here at this time for it is a force field that requires many to be conscious of their own light and power and to bring it forward to assist all on the planet and to assist the planet herself for balance. As the fear escalates on the planet and things lose their stability, we beings of light must hold true to what we know and remain grounded and steadfast for others. Those of us who are empathic will surely feel the fear of others, but we will know how to transmute rather than carry this fear. There will come a time when fear will be remembered as only an illusion, and we will know that existence is not only of the third dimensional level.

The sooner we can realize and accept this fact as truth the easier it will become for all of us to encompass the changes occurring on the planet, meeting them with the full understanding of our participation in them and knowing that the reason for our being here now is to accommodate these changes. We are here to release old ways and patterns of thinking and behavior that do not serve, to heal our past, present, and future and all simultaneous and parallel lives. Is it now time to make life simpler and to become more awake to our existence and purpose of being together now as a family of light and love.

These are big dramatic times on the planet now as never been experienced before. Yes mighty civilizations have come and gone many, many times over. However, this time is far different than ever before, as human evolution has come so far forward is now able to accept radical change and ascend to new dimensions and realms in full awareness of all of its beings. Much depends on one's individual viewpoint as to what shall come of it. For you are the creator of your thoughts and your own dynamics of life. As you venture ever so far forward you must also venture deeper, so much further within.

Life is full of twists and turns yet it becomes easier when one remains true to oneself with honor and love beyond measure.

As you begin to understand what is happening on Earth, you will come to more fully realize how important it is to remain centered and focused. It will be necessary to be totally aware of your thoughts and feelings and what you are conjuring up for yourself and those involved around you. To what extent and with what dynamics do you wish to experience that which you are thinking?

Manifestation is of thought and creation. Therefore, we are great Creators, instantly creating out of our own inner self. For it is of the universe within that creation comes forth, in and through all things. Look no further and search no longer for Prime Source outside of yourself nor clad within another. You are of God, One with God. Your truth is all encompassed within your very own soul; this truth of which you are in search of now.

Recognize and connect with that soul part of yourself on a deep level of communication in Spirit. Know yourself from only this part that is your own true Self for within that core of Self is your intuition, desires, and divinity, all that ever was and ever will be. The Divine Self of the Creator and you are entwined inexplicably. You are forever one with Source and with all things seen and unseen. This will be revealed to you forever in the true aspect of being with the Creator in an existence of life and love beyond your wildest comprehension.

This new energy that you are experiencing is of Prime Source and is of instant manifestation and consciousness of thought. It is here now for everyone to use and to be creative with. It is a thinking energy and, therefore, vital that you monitor your thoughts and feelings in order to create what you desire for your highest good. God Source is the energy of all things and, thus, this photon energy is of the great oneness and of the beyond. Universal in scope and of such great magnitude is that all will be affected by its predominance on the planet. It is here to stay and will affect every area of our domain, not only that of Mother Earth but of each of our physical structures as well. This new energy will prove to be far superior to anything we have had available to us previously on the planet, and thus it will afford us ample opportunity to create that which we need most to advance our civilization and quicken the senses.

Some of us have already achieved much in adjusting to this new energy and its resourcefulness, and are quite adept at feeling its vibrations. As more souls advance, many more souls will realize the old tendency to hold onto thoughts as if there will never be another, circulating them as in a tumbler where they always resurface and confront us.

This is particularly true with a negative thought. Once it has completed its purpose, it must be discarded and not allowed to regenerate. Otherwise, it feeds upon itself and forms a circular pattern, coming back to meet itself with the thinker in the midst of its circular motions. Such thoughts can spiral up or down according to the energy given to them.

If you can become an observer of yourself and lift your awareness to a higher level of light or understanding and give no energy to negative thoughts, you will see that the emotion attached to the thought no longer has a hold over you. Then, when the thought has nothing to grasp, its energy will dissipate of its own accord. In that moment, if you allow yourself to feel the vastness of your conscious mind, you will come to realize how much more of you there is to experience. You will realize how grand an opportunity is afforded for you to move beyond all that is holding you back, all that you no longer need to satisfy old patterns.

Your Soul is the finer part of who you are. It desires you to connect with it on a deeper level. The more you can release, surrender, and forgive yourself the more free you will become and the more able you will be to experience the Soul energy from a place of God's unconditional love.

Prayer for God's Children of Earth

Beloved Father-Mother God, how humbled we are to know we are created in your image, in your light, love, and magnificence. Now is the unfolding of that Life of the Christ, of pure Light and Love. Beloved One, how can we best accommodate you? How can we best advance the planet to reach her pinnacle of pure radiance? How can we reach the thousand years of peace, Beloved Father? We, as humble human beings, have this extraordinary opportunity to be all who you have proposed us to be. We are the co-creators with God. We are your God Children, your instruments for change. We are the bearers of Light and upliftment for all life everywhere. We are extraordinary beings in our human embodiment, loving, caring, and forever in search of Truth. We are who you know us to be; the Gods and Goddesses who walk the Earth that all life may exist in lasting peace.

AMEN

CHAPTER VII

Life in the Father

There comes a time in each person's life when we realize there is much more than this third-dimensional self. In that awareness, we are able to better understand the true love of God and everlasting life. When people can comprehend reincarnation as an actual fact and realize that they have lived on this Earth sphere many lifetimes, they will suddenly expand their own awareness.

Dear children, do you not feel this as part of your own truth? Have you not journeyed this way many lifetimes hence and before? Why then is it so difficult to comprehend this as the marvelous truth of God for His children?

In truth, life is Eternal as it has been decreed by God forever and ever more!

Thus it is so! Thus it forever will be! God has bequeathed upon each soul a life through all eternity in all of its varied forms and in whatever level of consciousness that is desirous of your own making. Is it now not a wonderful and profound idea to have this acknowledgement of life forever lasting and the Oneness of all things?

What of the Father? Is He not the biggest part of who you are? Is He not that part who speaks to you ever so softly, ever so lovingly? Listen now for that still small voice that comes to you ever so softly and gently. I sayeth to you this day; it is the Father who you hear! It is the Father who you feel! It

is the Father who shows you the way, ever so protective of His children! It is He who speaks to you through your heart center and through your vibration of love upon this planet.

The Father-Mother God brings this information to you so that you will appreciate yourself ever more profoundly and acknowledge that part of your- self who is beholden to Him, the life stream that is ever pouring forth from your being that sustains you in the flesh, in the body, and in the feeling and heart center of your being through the essence of your spirit and soul! It is the great conscious awareness playing with your heartstrings that tugs at you to hearken and listen to these words now.

The words are for you to read, to hear, and to absorb into your being, to meditate upon, to recognize the truth they speak to you this day and always! The time is now, my beloveds, to realize how much your Creator loves you, how much you are cherished and adored! In this life we are privileged to walk upon the Earth and to experience all that God has for us in His great wealth and abundance, limitless and pure. I urge you now to know this as your truth and to accept it as your own. Through acceptance you can fully realize your potential and creativeness, to utilize the highest potential as a hu-man (God-man) being in the fullness of life at this expanse of time.

Your Creator loves you unconditionally and forever, Your Creator is operating through you at all times in all ways. Your Divine Self is your divinity. Through your divinity this aspect of yourself exists! Contact God within.

Look within, not without, for your source. Look not above, for it is not there. Look instead to the greatest part of your soul. Look at your own being that you may be still to hear, feel, and receive this great gift of divinity! Bring it closer to your awareness and existence to live each breath in the purity of the Divine Self. Seek not that of the outer world but rather seek the Father's counterpart remaining within. It is time to recognize that part of your dominion and claim it! By claiming it and giving no person jurisdiction over it, you are then empowered to be that perfection of the God-Goddess so created in the likeness and image of God!

We have never been exposed to this radiance and potential until now for we were not ready to accept such magnificence. Imagine the joy and love to be experienced once we have released all that is of the old perspective. Coming to realize what is reality and what is an illusion. Looking forward to the reality that none of it was true and that we have all been held apart from our total self for these many centuries. Now it's time for our undoing of this barrier that we may experience our fullness, our radiant love of God, and our very own Divinity within!

It is there, becoming ever more profound as we recognize that part of ourselves. We are becoming aware of our potential and how it feels to be Divine Beings. We are the 'I AM' Gods of the universe! This is not a selfish thing but our true heritage, our birthright to be the absolute most that we can be and choose to be! "I and the Father are One" is not a false statement nor are they mere words! Truth is very much alive today as it was when stated; we only need to claim it. This is true and this is NOW!

Stretch your imagination now and envision this new modality of life.

Envision living on Earth with her heightened vibration, her new energy, and her dynamic of living where nothing is needed but of our own thought of creation. Imagine a heavenly consciousness of everything, with no need for all the rudiments of this third dimensional reality. When you do, the present way of being will seem as antiquated as our forefather's way of transportation with horse and buggy.

By our sheer will and the Grand Design of God we will acquire all of this potential that spearheads us into this evolutionary process. God is love! The world that He formulated enables us to be all who He is, and this world is everlasting and forever more! We, as a populace, must be willing to allow for creation to come forth to present Self in the magnitude of all that is in the Glory of Prime Source and of all things!

What shall we create for ourselves now? What of this? Is it of us that we do the work, or is it God's desire for us? Would it be now that you surrender to your own God Self and the Love your Creator has for you, accepting your own Divinity in order to build the creations of your future Self! Proud Beings we are, with an ego that wants recognition. All of this must be released into the nothingness that we can experience NOW, that is and always shall be of God. Feel the wonderment of it, the power and the beauty of creation, in and of itself. Fear not for this is the design of you, the design of your Creator, and the journey we have all agreed to undertake at this time for the benefit of the world and the future of all mankind.

The quality of love God has for His children is not of this Third Dimension but of all dimensions. God's love is forever eternally gifted to His children in form or formlessness, self-sustaining and enlightening, never to be withheld in the magnificence of the Oneness of all things! Is this not true? We are unaware of our magnificence. How great and gifted we are as souls embodied now in this new energy of love that is fully incorporated within our heart.

There are no limitations or obstructions for all are abundant and pure and available through the process of love, the process of receiving our good. It is not God who withholds anything from His children nor would He ever for He is omniscient, omnipresent, omnipotent within and through all!

As you release your Divine self into the spirit of your own soul, you will experience the dynamic of God's love for you, His child, ever expanding and growing like a garden well-tended to flourish with tender loving care amidst the chaotic world in which we live but whose soul sits astride the greatest force of life energy ever brought forth for mankind. Hear His voice and revel in it! How beautiful. What an extraordinary gift to this world now.

You are like a baby awakening in the Father's motherly arms of love, knowing and feeling this great opening and awareness of change, awareness of a love so magnificent that it's indescribable! This love holds one to another and courses through all particles and atoms erasing all negativity and shadow. In the Light of the Christ, there is no darkness. The Christed Light is pure light and pure energy from Prime Source so Divine and energetic, constantly flowing and increasing as we are made aware of and recognize it. This Christed Light is not for one only but available to the all. Thus, you need only to believe and receive. As your heart is opened to love yourself most dearly as a beloved soul, you are then freed of all the limitation and stigma of your many lifetimes.

It is a new garment, the Essence of the Divine, the essence of pure radiance, love, and peace in which one is cloaked. Nothing can tamper nor penetrate this new garment of the Father because it is the seamless garment of the bride and its contents are pure and whole and complete! The one so clothed is forever maintained in the Light of the Christ and, thus, is forever within the conscious level of His love.

In the richness of life is the form of the Creator's love for us. Through living in all its complexity and trials we reach the level of understanding of His love for us. There is not a moment that He is not there for us. Reach and grasp, and you shall have His hand ever clasped within yours! Rest and He shall rest beside your soul. Come as little children and let Him cherish the soul who you are.

We have been so graced, Beloved Father, so deeply graced and loved. The depth of the ocean and the expanse of the journey begins with us. There is nothing else neither whence we come nor whence we go but that of our soul, which is the Truth and the essence of our being in conscious awareness, en- lightened in the Glory of His name and endowed with life everlasting as gifted from God. Neither a grain of sand nor a blink of a star nor a twist of a leaf is without this great Oneness of Spirit. Nothing else exists save for that which God created in His great love for His own Consciousness.

The love of God is so pure it is forever a beacon to call His children Home to the place from whence they came. At that moment of full reconciliation of our Being, there is no separation. Over the eons of time, we have become ever more separated and alone. Loneliness is causing great grief for many and will become greater yet as people become very depressed in their emotional bodies. Control, for centuries, has caused individuals to lose the connection to their true Being-ness. We have separated as a society to such a degree that there is little room for love or anything new and different. We are all one race, that of God, as are all life forms, including the animal, plant, and elemental kingdoms.

As you become more aware of the Father's Divine Self, communication with Him will become ever more prevalent and stronger. Suddenly, you will be One with His love. Through that love, the phenomenal self enlarges His soul, and your Soul, in turn, receives His incomprehensible Love until both are merged in totality as One. Such is this integration of the Christ Spirit and the dynamics of living life through this aspect of Self. Imagine yourself, if you will, on a grander scale so incredibly mired with the Oneness of all that

nothing is separate or outside the realm of possibilities. Thus, you can create a beautiful existence for yourself.

How do you maintain a quality of self-acceptance and love? By opening your heart and soul to that which resides inside and to realize this is how to commune with God. There is not a "you" and an "I." There is only *One,* and that Oneness is the gift of the loving Father's idea of life, the unfolding One- ness throughout all existence. Whether of animal or plant, inanimate or living, the subatomic structure remains the same throughout all things, based on the energy so given by God's Love for us. This love is to be recognized on a soul level. However, it has to be accepted as a conscious part of our makeup, our humanness, and ignited within in order for us to consciously be aware of Its Presence.

You are that for which you are seeking! There is no other place to look or go but that of your own self-contained being within. Stop seeking for that which appears to be unobtainable from without, but rather learn to listen quietly from within and then surrender that which you seek to God and be open to receive that which He has for you.

Follow that which you are guided to be or do, trusting His guidance, trusting your own truth. Do you not see the dynamics, the power of this potential within? All is from Source, all is Absolute, and all is of God!

There is no one-way! All ways lead to God because each way comes from within the heart and soul of each being who was ever created by the Father through His great love of His God child. Our individual searches will continue, as they have for these many millennia, until we become open enough and surrender enough to accept God's Truth!

There have been many who have come to Earth as Messiahs to teach His doctrine. Words have been said and spoken beholden unto Him. Words have been misinterpreted in the many times since these beloved Messiahs—Buddha, Mohammad, Krishna, Jesus, and others—walked the Earth.

God's Word has come forth by the many sent here to enlighten us, to transform us, to have us hear that which was spoken. These Messiahs spoke messages for our good. But their words have been misinterpreted and often not understood. You are here to reinterpret the good, to live the truths, these Divine Principles of life, to come closer to the Father's Being as you grasp the knowledge of His Divinity, His Love, and His Being. You cannot help but to yield to your own calling and divine self, ever powerful, ever loving, and ever true unto your soul's journey.

Is your calling not the same as the Creator's calling for you? Are you not the same as your Creator? Thus, if you judge another, are you not judging your Creator as well? How do you know that you, in a previous lifetime, haven't traversed the same journey as the person you're judging in this lifetime? Consider that the person is a catalyst for your soul to advance and that you are also a catalyst for the advancement of the other person's soul.

Without sorrow would you fully comprehend the exuberance of joy?

Without a beloved's heart leaving or changing would you not know the pain of loss and the joy of reunion? Earth is an arena for human emotions that hold the fabric of our being intact, emotions that open our hearts to aspects of self we dare not to feel? Each human's soul is responsible to feel its own emotions and pain. Our feeling and emotions are of vital importance to experience our own growth by, to learn by them and to move through them with the knowledge that they are the greatest asset to our life's experience on Earth. They are not to dismiss but rather to look at and feel the emotions on a deep level to gain the understanding from them and to heal.

We are given the opportunity by God to ascend to another dimension while Earth experiences all of the transformation on the third dimensional level. Jesus said that we cannot enter the kingdom of heaven but as a child. Thus, an innocent child we shall come. And, thus, we let go of all good, bad, and indifference in the sweet innocence of a baby.

In the sweet love of the Father, we will create for ourselves another existence that the Self-Realized have known of and been in, a sweet existence of perfect peace, love, joy, and harmony. We shall traverse the universes and be unlimited ever more! Such is the opportunity given by God to Jesus, His only begotten Son who led the way for us to transform our vibration into the Christ Light. That gift has always been available to us, but only now are we becoming aware of our power to use it. Therefore, now is the time for this evolutionary change on Earth. How great it is! Such a beautiful gift given solely for God's children through the Christ who planted the seed two thou- sand years ago!

The promise was made as it was so chosen by humankind, a promise for peace that surpasses all understanding, a peace to last for a thousand years. Thus, it is the gift of God for His children that we have asked for millennia, this peace, love, and joy. Now soon to come and soon to be embellished upon the Earth in such a way many will think it's the end time, while others will see only the appropriateness of all that is transpiring. The time is now for this evaluation, for looking at ourselves deeply in order to release all that no longer serves.

Yes, this is quite a ride up and down with many emotions, surfing the wave as it crests and falls, riding the currents as they pull back and surge ahead. It is a time of much turmoil of thoughts and feelings, a time when we can address that which is believed to be ours, and let go of what doesn't serve before we come face to face with God.

This is a time of great transformation, both on an Earthly level and within our own conscious being. This is a great time for all to be awakened and to accept our own divinity, knowing we are more than we appear to be. Many are in fear, not knowing what to expect, as so much negativity has been presented concerning all the prophecies and legends. Much dismay and negative thinking has led us to believe God has somehow allowed all this to happen and has abandoned us.

In reality, those who suffer this way have abandoned themselves. It is, thus, necessary for God to intervene and have His own magnificent plan now come to the fore. Those who are in fear of the current state of affairs are under false belief for we have all been misled for many centuries concerning the truth. Religions propagated much falsehood in order to induce mankind to give its power away, thinking there was a need to be controlled.

It is now a time when all falsehood will be revealed, and many will be challenged within their own belief systems. It is a time of revelations when the truth will be revealed. The people of the Light shall come forth. The Dead Sea Scrolls will bring forward much information that has been hidden from history, and this will cause a great re-evaluation within our belief systems.

It is important that we receive this information now, in order that the souls who wish to accept their divinity be prepared. The Decree of God is that the time now at hand should come. Were it not for God, humanity would have annihilated itself years ago. Yet, here we are today and here we will be tomorrow if we wish to continue further. Our spiritual DNA is now being re-created as it was originally meant to be, allowing us access to all that is our true nature.

Those who have chosen to be here to accommodate the shift in consciousness will increase their level of awareness to such a degree that all beings may reach a level of heightened awareness. Many will be heralded to come forth to assist those who are in need of understanding the expansion. So now is the advent of the new-ancient age, one of perfect enlightenment and truth.

Come now and listen with an open heart and mind that we may be brought to the point of a deeper understanding of our own Divine Self of the Christ within. Come unto this day and let us open our hearts to receive all that the Father has for us, my beloveds. Come and learn of His love for is it not the Father's House in which we live, is it not His love that is all around us? The beat of our heart is the beat of His heart at the fountain of our soul. Our existence is through the Light of God and by no other means. The closer we hold Him to ourselves the closer He holds us and the dearer we become to one another. It can be no other way for this is the promise of eternal life forever and ever. Thus, we will no longer be the mere image of who we are but the grander image of all that is and ever will be! The more we can grasp this understanding the more we can open to the full awareness of our own capacity to re-ignite the soul of the Christ within.

Come now and stand this day in the full Presence of the Lord. At this most profound of all times, He is asking us to join in the evolution of the plan- et that we may all transform that which was into something far more beautiful than we ever imagined. So why do we hang on so tightly to the past? Why do we not release our fears unto Him, knowing He is our protector and guide in all life? Come this day and rethink that of which you perceive yourself to be, for you are much more than you ever have conceived possible. It is a powerful and enlightening experience to accept this truth and to live by it daily, to understand it fully in your Beingness. Come now and grasp this realization to your heart and soul to live limitless and free from your own bondage.

At this time, we are asked to come forward and accept this truth of our Divine Self that is our birthright. Come now and let our love be known and do not hesitate to be in full openness that the heart may shine from within and be the healing light needed on the planet. Our light is of the utmost importance now to ignite the spark of love within the human consciousness, causing the energy patterns to evolve swiftly. Love yourself and others without condition. God requests that we open our heart and soul to the greater good of living who we are as individual beings on a spiritual journey. This we must do for the evolution of mankind to move forward.

The Father's House is full of wonder and beautiful gifts for mankind that have been unavailable for too long. Thus at this time of planetary evolution it is His fondest desire for us to accept our responsibility to be the God children who we are, to recognize His unconditional love and allow that love to come through us as His vehicles for change. We are now transitioning to a new level of being, a new awareness of God as not being outside of ourselves. Rather God is very close and dear to our hearts and resides at the very core of our being. There are many who desire drama to make them realize their God Self, yet it's not necessary to enact drama in order to know the divinity within. For with subtlety, powerful seeds for change can be planted and thus in subtle ways much is accomplished in a deep and profound way.

Prayer

We are beholden unto the Father for all our lifetimes and His great love for us. Ever so closely do we hold Him in our hearts and ever so closely are we One. This we know to be the Truth of the great recognition of Source within. Our desire is to integrate into the One, with a joy-filled heart, where there is no separation perceived on any level.

AMEN

CHAPTER VIII

Claiming Our Divinity

When each person realizes the truth of his or her being and takes possession of it, we will no longer be under the illusion of control by others. Rather, we will henceforth remain within our own powerful Source and will stand upright amidst all men and enjoy the flavor of ownership of this Divine Self, that part of our being that is the substance of all life and all lifetimes. This divinity of self has been forfeited by way of our own folly and misconception of what has been given to humanity as truth for centuries. So many untruths have been imbedded into our conscious thought, as our daily bread, that it's difficult to discern another possibility of truth, one taught by so many Masters for so many lifetimes one after another, and yet again repeated. Buddha, Jesus, Mohammed, Krishna, Mary and Quan Yin, and others have all brought forth the same message, calling the children of God awaken!

Is there not a great longing for that eternal part of ourselves to be rediscovered, reunited, and returned home to God? Is that not what we all are longing? We are able to recognize the greatness of this achievement of our being, opening to receive God's pure non-judgmental love for His children. Eternally, claim your divinity, claim for yourself your birthright as a God Child.

Lay claim to all that the Father has in His House. Claim your inheritance and your possession of the greatest gift that all mankind could ever desire, want, or need, expressed through your core being in the minutest and most dynamic way possible, through your Divine Self, your soul self who has traveled with you all of your lifetimes since the creation of who you are and you separated from the Father! This is your total birthright, your legitimate Self, made in the likeness and image of God, the all perfect, whole, and complete you within and through yourself through all eternal lives. You are a God child of such ability, of such light and love that nothing on Earth can replicate the delicate manner by which the Father created each soul.

Your soul is the greater part of Self, a Divine Spark from our Creator and the true aspect of all who you are, ever were, and ever will be. This is the single reason you are here today for it's the soul's journey into the visible and invisible whereby all is possible according to Divine Law. Thus, the soul is the God of Gods, the I AM THAT I AM! It is God's richness of Being and The Tapestry of Life as it ebbs and flows forth from your soul! How powerful and yet how demure.

The soul is longing to be acknowledged, longing to be fully present in all of the dynamics of the Creator in bodily form, ever present, ever guiding and directing us to aspire to the greatness of our truth. How wonderful it is to have this soul aspect as to who we really are in life everlasting for eternity and to build and expand upon and bring this one-of-a-kind soul, in its uniqueness of Being, into each lifetime. How wonderful to experience each degree of life in this dynamic form on Earth absorbing the wisdom and the challenges of growth through all lessons encountered while traveling on the road to home with many stops along the way.

Our Being is all too engrossed in this third dimensional illusion to realize the full potential of the soul to experience, re-experience, or change the dynamic of each moment. Yet, we are beginning to realize the possibilities of an existence through our soul level of consciousness and awareness for all future potential. The dynamics of whatever we are creating at this particular moment catapults us forward into the creation of the future for each of us as individuals and as a collective. Thus, we live by what we create at all times in many diverse ways. We live by being aware of how powerful our mind is, of our mental process and thinking, by monitoring our thoughts to hear what they are stating to us. We are consciously aware of what is most beneficial to each other and mankind. We will not be wanting when all understand this deepest principle of truth and become one with it in all manifestation. When we claim our divinity, peace on Earth will be unheralded forever and mankind will be loved ultimately and forever.

The great drama of the past is now behind us, and a new day is now present when we can be sovereign unto ourselves as individuals, as countries and as a populace inhabiting this great planet. By expanding our belief to include the possibility of a new way of thinking, being, living, and breathing, we allow Earth to do the same. We attain all potential and possibilities of a grand and beautiful future by accepting our part in all of this, both positive and negative, by never holding fast to the old and creating new beliefs.

A new way is formed in the NOW (No Other Way) of existence as we live it and choose it to be at this very critical juncture in our planetary evolvement. It can be the most majestic and magnificent time ever in existence when all levels of reality are entwined for the betterment of humanity and for all life through the cohesive formulation of LOVE, that of our God Source and our own divinity.

Now is the time to regain our connection with Source that never left in the first place but was there all the time as we continued to look outside our- selves to build all of our beliefs, allowing our guidance to be stilled and shut down. All of our attention has been given to those who acted as if they held the correct belief and pathway, allowing us to be directed in their ways and beliefs. Thus, we are embedded and mired today, as nations and as a world, looking to others rather than acknowledging our own power. So indebted are we to the financial institutions of the world that we hardly have the opportunity to free ourselves from the encumbrances of what has been enacted in the name of good for us. This paradigm will no longer serve. All that has been created to control mankind, all that has been built in non-integrity, all that does not benefit humanity and is detrimental to existence will no longer be supported by that which is coming.

Thus, we must now unite our collective consciousness and come to the realization that we are *One!* We are the co-creators of what is in our universe, on our planet, and amongst our people. We created all of it in our delusion, in our false belief of what was true and best for us. Nonetheless, it is to be

re-evaluated and released in order to create anew that Golden Age that God has intended for His children. We shall be complete human beings with our entire spiritual DNA intact, existing in a diverse culture without any limitations instilled by others.

Christ-Consciousness

Christ-Consciousness is what we really are in our totality and in our living truth. The depth of Christ-Consciousness is of a magnitude so great and so profound that it is life everlasting and eternal. An extraordinary gift given by Prime Source has no recourse but to desire to return home to its Creator. Thus, we are continually in search of home, of God.

Rather than searching, as we have done forever on the outside, our soul now demands us to accept our divine heritage that is the Living Christ within! We are called to recognize our divinity, to become more aware of this wonderful disguised part of our Self that has been buried for so many lifetimes. As our soul counterpart becomes alive with the Spirit of Christ, then an aspect

of love that is so true, so sweet, and so gentle fills our cup to overflowing and brings a greater sense of Self and a peaceful way of existence that has never been experienced to this extent within our consciousness.

This is the dynamic of the Christed Energy, the birth of the Christ within that is not a phenomenon out there beyond us, but is truly right within our very core of being! Each cell responds to this loving essence of

Christ Energy as we call upon it and incorporate it within our whole and true being. This Christed-Energy is the most profound and powerful energy on earth and comes from Christ directly. Realize you are divine, awakening to the point you actually feel the Divine flowing through you. Allowing the anxiety and fear to dissipate into nothingness as you are enveloped in the essence of the Divine Love. Regardless of your situation or what you are doing in the present moment, you are divinely blessed. We are never to stray again to that which we believe to be outside of ourselves but rather follow what our heart and soul has designed for us.

We have long given credence to outside circumstances, to events that herald a way of thinking that is not always of our Highest Good or of God's liking. Thus, we must connect deeply with our own inner being, our own God Self, paying closer attention to each vibration that registers in either positive or negative feelings. In our awareness, our soul knows what is best and will guide us to whatever heightens us into our Spirit, to wherever or whatever we, by the grace of God, are to do next or with whom we are to be involved.

We, as humans, may believe we have control of the rudder, though for many centuries we have just been following what has been programmed into us. In this century, this millennium, there appeared a crevice between the physical world and the spiritual world that has grown ever so wide and deep. Rectification of this rift is the promise of the future for, as the bridge to tomorrow takes us from this dynamic to the next, the consciousness of humanity will shift.

Some will move forward in their evolution with planet Earth, while many will choose to leave the Earth plane not wanting to experience all the changes nor that of the Earths. They will be of greater assistance to us from the other side. There are those who are beginning to feel this shift and are very receptive to it, and there are those who are panicked and do not know what to do with it.

Being in total fear of whatever they are feeling, many do not want to address their feelings. These are the populace who increasingly live in fear and terror. Sadly, they have lost contact with God, with Prime Source, the Creator of love, which is the antithesis of fear. Having nothing to turn to but their beliefs of fear and separation, they mostly turn to and echo what is offered outside of themselves rather than looking inward. Those who seek outside themselves will no longer find peace nor be at peace for they are not able to see the answer of God's love. They do not believe or trust in God, but are continually seeking outside themselves rather than within.

All members of humanity are urged now to search within themselves and to recognize their fears, as well as their longing for God, their direct and true connection with the Creator. It's not easy to look within when fear and self-judgment are embedded there. Nevertheless, now is the time to be in sovereignty unto ourselves and in acknowledgement of our total being in Oneness with God. Thus, we are once again urged to capture that part of ourselves who has so long been forgotten and not relied upon.

Can you release the beliefs of tribal past conditioning long enough to accept that part of yourself who is of God? Can you open your heart to feel this Divine Essence within as part of your Divine Self?

What does this mean: "Your Divine Self?" It means the part of you who recognizes "Your" connection to Prime Creator with every atom of your being. It means that every part of "You" is every part of God and nothing is outside of that Divine Self. Your thought is God's thought and your manifestation is God's manifestation. You are of the whole and completeness of all things. Humanity is building a bridge to the new tomorrow, to the unification of all souls in full recognition of this unity and the framework of the Divine in all things, in full integrity of oneself and one another.

There will no longer be seeking outside but knowing we are of God, the great I AM THAT I AM. Thus, it passes and the day shall come when we are all operating under the umbrella of light and love, so extreme and energetically present that we will want nothing. Instantaneously, we shall manifest all that we need. Instantaneously, we shall have our bread on the table, our clothes provided.

The illusion of the third dimensional reality and its apparent limitations will no longer be but a fragment of our old imagination. The illusion always was purely an illusion, a dream made manifest by our individual and collective thought forms. With this realization, we transcend the darkness of night and step into the understanding of all that is available to us as children of God.

Come now. Would not the Father of all creation who created us as His God child bestow upon us *all* His gifts? Would the Father hold back anything from us in His pure joy and love of life in perfect abundance? Would He not lavishly surround us in His joy and beauty of all things, all nature, and all perfection?

Where the Father dwells there is no darkness. There is only the beauty of the Divine Self, the Holy One in pure essence of His Light. All is from the first cause. All is of creation. All is of wanting no-thing for the Source of all provides all.

But first we must have the desire for God's love for desire opens us to life, to searching for something more rather than the rudimentary daily round of existence. When we have the desire to live in the truth of spirit and in our Divine Self, becoming one with all things and one with the Father and the Christ who resides within, then we are lifted to a higher state of awareness, a vibration that is of the Golden Sun!

When this status is obtained, there is no need for lack, fear, transgression, or sorrow. When we understand and accept that we are of God and the Christ incarnate within, then our soul energy ignites the fire of the individual and the spark of the divine. Then we are whole unto ourselves.

Once ignited, it is a flame of an untold energy Source that expands and furthers us into higher understanding, into other realms, and opens us to all potential of life. As we expand our consciousness in this way, we see there is no returning to the other side of self. Our soul is now awake and very conscious of the journey and vibration of our atonement (at-one-ment) with Prime Source.

We are then taking a continual step to this Atonement. One step leads to another until we have reached the highest vibration of our Soul. Our embodiment is ever expanding and changing along with our conscious awareness. The cells within our body re-emerge with a memory of Prime Source and existence of other times and places. When jarred awake into our own truth of Self, we perceive our soul on a very deep level and, thus, we gradually merge and unite with Source in a very magnificent way!

Embracing the Christ within

You need not limit yourself in the pure consciousness of spirit for spirit is free and open and full of wonderment and love! Spirit is who you are! Spirit has no ownership, no boundaries, and no limits. Spirit is pure energy of life and of love. Through this love all creation is formed!

The more love essence we have, the more the universe will funnel energy through our embodiment. The final act of manifestation from Prime Source will enable us to feel this aspect of our self and know we are full of the Oneness of the Creator. This is pure existence, and it is here for our taking whenever we wish to call upon this Christed energy.

How simply this works and is made manifest when we believe and are open to allow ourselves to receive this aspect of the Creator as it flows in whatever manner is deemed possible. This energy is available for all to draw from. It is endless energy ever pouring forth, ever flowing, ever ebbing; to and fro, to and fro, encompassing all things. It is life in its fullest and most Holy form.

Do you want to simply exist, or do you want to exceed yourself and live life in your fullest capacity? The universal energy is there for you to draw upon and to sustain you on the planet at this time of incredible change. Find peace in this and know that the seed of the Christ within you is being brought forth. Revel in the understanding that you are at a depth you would have been unable to reach two thousand years ago.

Who instilled the memory of the cross and guilt and misery following the crucifixion of Christ into each man and woman alive then and now? Was it not His joy to live His life for us? Was it not His mission to teach and instill in us His love of the Father regardless of the trials and tribulations he experienced?

Jesus is with us to this day instilling that Love within us, and it is as strong today as it was then. He asks you to come forward now and recognize where humanity has been all this time! He asks you to see how misled we have been all these lifetimes and why we are back now to correct our wrong belief, to move into the dynamics of the consciousness of the Christed One as He lives, moves, and breathes amidst us.

Let us come as children in the full knowingness of this truth and His love for us, His great joy in our acceptance of these great truths. He standeth alone in His love of the Father. He standeth for All in His greatness of God, undefiled and unfettered by whatever humanity has bestowed for such a One is of God and He knows nothing else but the pure existence of love within. Jesus knows the essence of Self and the God child within all things, in all life as it was and ever shall be, life unto life, forever, eternally, and forevermore.

Can you not envision all systems of the universe also increasing and expanding in consciousness? The Masters who walked this Earth these many lifetimes want each of us to attain this level of the Christ Consciousness that they may exceed further and continue their work in the worlds that God has prepared for them. As we ascend to the level of attainment they have reached, so too are they allowed to reach heightened levels of existence for themselves. Life is not stagnant but an ever increasing energy of growth, movement, and attainment to bring forth new ideas and new ways to be, to experience and develop in all ways be it the body, mind, or soul. It is the soul's purpose to experience all aspects of the Soul Self. It is a continuous process for evolution never ends anywhere. Why should it, when we have a Creator of such magnitude and thought? It is His great pleasure to create and create again, ever creating with us in conjunction with Prime Source.

The Love of the Christ is amidst all now, becoming ever so stronger as we advance. Take it to your core essence for it's You! It is not outside you; it is deep within. It is your Divine Self, and it is for you to take ownership of now—if you choose—and ride the waves of change. You must take owner- ship of this love. You must take ownership of your own divinity, your own emotions, thought forms, and patterns. You must release all the old negative thought patterns and realize they no longer serve. The potential is everlasting, grand, and very beautiful as you reconnect with your real Self and every aspect of who you are. Become one with all, become that Divine Human Being, Divine Essence of your Creator!

The Christ Energy is contained within the seed of each individual soul. It is up to each one of us to receive this love, to open our hearts and cherish it for in so doing we honor God and His Eternal Love for us, His children. God is the Source and joy of all life! Would He keep the joy for Himself when it comes from His being? As Prime Creator, would He not share it and watch it grow?

It matters not in what realm you are, nor to what degree you experience this love. What matters is that you discover a profound love for Self in your deepest core being. Life is His Gift, and it is the Father's desire that His children have all things that bring them joy made manifest on Earth. Yet, we forestall the receiving of this love when we, in our humanness, never believe it is ours to receive. Instead, we pick up arms and do everything we can on Earth to judge this love, to defile it, or run from it or change the precept given by God. Then, in our humanness, wonder how God could so love the world that He would hold us in no harm's way, with no judgment and no discord, with only pure love, light, and the Divine Essence of Being.

God interacts with us in every breath of every day of our lives on Earth and then thereafter eternally. We are created from the Father and to the Father we shall return. How great a gift is that? How great a benefactor is He? God is the benevolence and the Oneness of all creation! He walks with us every day. He resides within the consciousness of each person in full knowing of all the light that shines forth from a baby's eyes or the smile on an elder's face. His children are one with the world! What more could a soul ask of God but to be One in His Love Divine! We will see a time when mankind accepts the Oneness of all creation.

We will open our hearts ever so wide and release our beliefs that have been holding us back from living this new energy, The Light of the Christ As each person becomes ever more aware of this LOVE, our heart and soul will become much more connected with this expression of Christ Consciousness.

We have arrived at this point of time where the Christ Consciousness can be lived and experienced, and we can be carried to the same awareness as that of Jesus 2000 years ago. We are able to transmute in the same fashion as He did into the realms of other dimensions and heightened vibration, which is as it should have been so long ago. But mankind was not ready or able to comprehend the gift until now. Now is the time for the awareness of consciousness to come forth and for us to wrap ourselves around the possibility for the greatest changes ever in the evolution of mankind and the planet.

If you will allow yourself to reach into your encodements, you will come to the full knowledge of this mighty plan and your part in it. Through the arrival of your being at this time on Earth this new energy is brought forth, to bring the Glory of the Lord into the breath of each soul and to awaken the heart through LOVE!

Certainly it will be challenging for some, as they do not know of this love nor understand how powerful, dynamic, and pure it is. As you release and do the work and find a non-identity within, you allow a space to be created of pure love, pure spirit, and pure light. Each must enter this void of no-thing to relinquish all that was believed to be of our identity. Through this non-identity new creation is formed and the soul is set free.

God is eager for us to come to Him now in this freedom of being in the Light of the Christ, to be that of which we were born to be, of which God has so given. We are each the spark, the soul coming to experience all of Him in every form with free choice and free will. Thus, at this time the Father is calling us home, to no longer be in the negative energies that beleaguer us.

Come, children of God and of the universe. Come this time to a new world and a new aspect of yourself. Come, children of the Earth, to a new awareness of The Golden Age with experiences so profound that all will be transformed in the twinkling of an eye. Come, that we shall live in harmony, peace, joy, and with beauty beyond our wildest expectations. This day it is asked of each of us to go deeper into the essence of our being in the Light of the Christ, the Light and Love of God, our Creator, and the possibilities for life in the Age of Aquarius.

Circumstances that prevail on our planet now cause some disturbance with the direction our planet Earth is heading into currently. Therefore, God, Prime Source, Allah has implemented a grander design for our great Mother Earth and those who reside thereon.

These changes must take place in the highest way possible for all souls everywhere and in full recognition of what we seek to create in alliance with God. It is not some mere whim that Prime Source has decided to have radical changes come about on the planet, nor is it simply just for our planet. This change involves all universes for all time and for all of creation. Thus the position we are in on Earth is pivotal in the overall expansion that is taking place and the new dimension we are entering. We are vibrating ever forward as a planet, and we earthlings will be very much stretched to expand in our own individual realities to accommodate a radical shift in perception. It is of such a grand magnitude that it has never been accomplished in the history of all worlds and universes! Thus all beings everywhere will recognize this great change with Earth and our galactic allies.

Earth is moving forward at an ever-increasing rate and will be cleansing and clearing her own organism. Earth will be more sustaining of life, more beautiful than ever. No one will be abandoned by our Creator, but we will be tested most assuredly. It is the Father's hope for all humanity to move with His plan and that of the other Councils who govern and balance the universes.

In her evolutionary process, the Earth will attain full enlightenment and conscious awareness within the coming years. This she will do for it's God's promise to her. She has carried humanity as far as she can at this time and, thus, as a living organism, is able to no longer sustain the negativity placed upon her. She will be traveling into another orbit, another direction where- by all who have caused her great harm in her attempt to sustain life will be cleansed and purified. Through this, we, as mankind, shall also be cleansing our souls and reconnecting with all who we are on every level, every cell, and every life through all lifetimes lived on Earth and elsewhere.

Never has there been such awareness and light as filtered unto this planet at this time. The light filaments coming through the grids pertain to every one of us. They infiltrate our being as we are open energetically to receive them. Thus, we are able to restructure our spiritual DNA, our cellular structure, our core essence, and our mind, heart, and soul. This we have accomplished by being open to change and by recognizing that we are more than mortal beings.

Our bodies are more than the physical structures we believe them to be.

They are our temples for our soul. We are carriers of light and the encodements of our Creator.

Thus, it is a time of great restructuring. Prime Creator is waiting for our acceptance of His Love, His Credence to give to us all that He has and all that He so desires. Would you not choose this for yourself? Would your heart be so closed you would not want to receive His great LOVE for you?

Beloveds, this choice comes to us now that we may go within deeper than we have ever gone. Meditate, soul search, realize the depth of your being!

Know you are a God child and accept your own Divine Self now! *It's the reunion with Self, and Self is God!*

Prayer

Beloved Father, as we become ever more aware of who we are as your divine beloveds, we come to full awareness and conscious of your Light, your untold Truth for us, your Love that traverses within every cell of our Being, in and through our Sacred Heart center and all life.

May we come to more fully understand this Gift of Life in all of the pure radiance of our Soul, on every level and in every essence of our Being. Truly, we are who You are! We are the beloved co-creators of our existence in this life and all life for there is no separation.

I AM THAT I AM.

AMEN

CHAPTER IX

Civilization Rises Anew

The Great Master Teacher, Jesus of Nazareth, planted the seed over two thousand years ago that would herald The Thirteenth Rise of Civilization that is now upon us. This new civilization is based upon that of the Thirteenth Disciple, the Master Jesus, and His teachings and His great lessons of Truth. His very words have contained the seed of this present time within them for these two thousand years, though misinterpreted and much abused. There is much truth coming forth now in all aspects of this Master Soul, the One sent to Earth to create for us a time-space whereby we could finally understand His message that has been shared with us over and over. He now brings forth this message within the soul of each human, the Truth spoken by Master Jesus in His ever-expanding Christ-Consciousness.

We have journeyed far to reach this level of creation, and we are now able to communicate more readily with other dimensions and believe in other possibilities that may exist. We are currently honored from all levels on High because we have chosen to partake of Christ-Consciousness, allowing it to germinate within our souls.

As we embark further on this road of discovery, much will be made known to us and much will be discovered. We shall gain a greater understanding of life on Earth and the creation of life itself. The Master Plan will carry us forward to release and cleanse all fear, false beliefs, manipulation, and control. We would possibly be terrified were we not forewarned. But we have been given the tools to operate with the understanding of going within. Therefore, we are grateful and benevolent for this occurrence as we journey into the unknown.

We will discover that Earth will, once again, become the pristine planet she was intended to be, and those who reside on her will, once again, become pristine in their own right. Together, all will be miraculously and gloriously shining in the light of a new rebirth and new dwelling. God has decreed at this time of human evolution an expansive state of growth as we fulfill His Grand Plan.

There will be no manipulation, control, rules, and regulations that, now, have reached the point where people cannot function. There will be no strife against one another as a populace, as a global society, as humanity. Rather, we will recognize that we are all connected and of the same life force essence of our Creator. We will realize the ONENESS of all life. As we arrive at this new level of Christ-Consciousness, we will experience a depth of our divinity which will lead us into our Great I AM Presence, that of God. As others become aware of their own Divinity, there will be an arising of the mass consciousness to afford us the opportunity to reach the level of the Christ-Consciousness that Master Jesus embodied.

There is little time left for this third dimensional reality to exist as it is. Thus, we are being compelled to develop what is most needed and what will benefit us during this transitional time. The full capacity of our cellular memory will be available to us and our brain will operate at full capacity. We will be multidimensional souls with total recall of all our lives. We will be able to exist in other dimensions and be of service to all those in need of our expertise and we theirs.

This transformation will have nothing to do with the ego. Rather, our Ascension is a spiritual phenomenon whereby we will enter into the full realm of the Masters and Angels who are constantly with us. God will open the door to all of the realms so that we may be more of an asset to

His Grand Plan.

Other sentient Beings throughout the universe are silently observing us as to our choices and how we are all going to handle this dimensional Shift.

Now is the time to educate one another here on Earth, to bring the knowledge forth regarding stewardship of Earth and to allow her the freedom to expand and become a gem in all the galaxy. No longer will she be in the dark but in her full glory and awareness of self. What a crowning achievement will have transpired! What a jewel, indeed, she will become!

In the next few years, we will find life to be more beautiful and joy-filled as each person works together to achieve a common purpose in life. It is this that God desires to experience through each of us as the image of His Divine Self.

With the concept of duality eliminated in the higher dimensions, we will be able to concentrate on what brings us joy, love, and light in a greater means of development and expansion. For this reason God has decided to proceed now with this movement, this energy that facilitates moving into other dimensions.

Earth will be the experiment of the ages, such that all other universes are gathering around to observe how her ascension can be accomplished through our love of Earth and our desire to assist her through this process. The work humans are accomplishing now is changing our entire encodements and essence beyond what has ever been witnessed previously. There is potential of such advancement that we would find ourselves catapulted into another aspect of life in a blink of an eye. Indeed, without our commitment to assist with the conscious thought of Love through these changes there could be complete disaster. The entire planet Earth would not be able to exist without our faith and knowing that she, too, can succeed with what she chooses to do at this time. How grateful she is for this. How indebted to the earthlings that are supportive to her and filled with her essence.

We now experience inter-connectedness on very deep levels that have heretofore not been experienced. We are awakening within to an inert strength that we have held hostage for many eons to such a degree that we have forgotten there was such a resource. Now we are opening fully to our entire being, our Soul essence, and all that is contained within.

This is inclusive as to the development of the DNA strands that have been withheld from us for so many centuries. Now it has been decreed by God to release these strands, to catapult us all forward into His Grand Design for who we are and why we are here now to serve those of the planet Earth, the Great Mother who herself is expanding in consciousness, moving into new dimensions in experience of the Light.

The New Earth is a safe haven for those who are ready and willing to travel such a journey. She is so full of the essence of life and so brimming with extraordinary gifts that we have only begun to seemingly experience it. This will entail all the great cities of which we have heard and dreamed and all the life contained within. It will be a Garden of Eden, so to speak. But first, in order to reach that level of spiritual awareness, we must traverse our own interior to really discover who lives there within. We must know that life in this new civilization is far beyond our wildest conception of anything we have accomplished so far in the history of this great planet for we are becoming the extraordinary NOW (No Other Way)!

God's blessing, bestowed upon us, is to accept all that He has waiting for us in His Kingdom and to partake of it as His blessed children! The Father and I are one, as are you, God Children, as are you! It's our birthright and His decree that we accept this as our own and to become that of which we are, The Divine Self, which is all encompassing of all universes, part of every atom and particle everywhere.

Life teems with the expectancy of this transformation and with the heightened sense and intensity that we are all experiencing within body, mind, and soul moving into this new evolution of civilization. How beautiful, how profound, and how joyful it is! It is our Father's pleasure to accept us into His House, which we never left but of our own consciousness. He has waited for our return as we come unto Him now. We are reunited as One with our Source, the greater part of ourselves, the I AM THAT I AM!

There is a deep longing inside for our Source, our sense of being more than we are, our recognition that we are spiritual beings on this great journey together and shall return one day to the Divine Spirit of our beloved Creator!

What joy and comfort we experience in this recognition in its truest sense of purpose as we move ever forward in our evolution and experience of that which is to come. How richly blessed we are, indeed, to be living on this beloved planet at this time, to experience all that we have come to experience for the Soul's purpose of life teachings and attainment of truth.

May we welcome the heightened awareness and new state of Being, living in constant communication with Father-Mother God, seeking none else but Prime Source and His everlasting Love for us! It is time, dear ones, time for us to come forward to accept our Divinity and become One with it, letting it lead us home. Let it lead us to build a new civilization, one of greater heights and realms of which we have only begun to perceive.

As Earth is in her evolutionary process and moving ever so fast into her dimensional shift, we are experiencing the challenge of having to rid ourselves of all of these false beliefs, all of that which is untrue and no longer supports us. We are experiencing the most profound clearing and cleansing ever on this planet and all planetary evolvements.

Our Creator has deemed this Decree at this time of human evolution. Yes, free choice has been given! Free will is an absolute that will always remain with us for it is His promise to us. Nonetheless, by this Decree of God, delivered through the Christ and all planetary structures heralded from the future, we, our human consciousness, and even Mother Earth are now in an expansive state of growth. The latitude allowed for this expansion is one unprecedented on Earth as never been heralded on any scale.

Thus, we are called now to be more aware of our thoughts and feelings and to patrol them diligently. Feelings are of major importance! Our feelings wrapped around our thoughts manifest what we are creating for ourselves, whether that of positive or negative experiences in our lives. People are often unaware that their feelings are of importance on a spiritual level, but the Di- vine Law of Feelings encompassed with our thoughts, form our outer reality. To create a world of profound peace and love, we must relegate to the rear that which no longer supports or sustains us as people on this planet. None of the old will be able to operate in the new energies coming forth. The new dimensions that Earth is moving into are those of a much-heightened awareness, of pure light and love of Prime Source.

No darkness, negativity, or duality will be supported. All will be only of pure light, love, joy, and peace! All will be of The Golden Age when consciousness is of oneness and togetherness, supportive of each other through conscious choice. Those who wish to derogate others, to spew their energies of negativity or control upon the many of this planet, to plague people with their ownership of one another will no longer be able to support themselves energetically. Whatever exploitation took place previously will no longer be sustained by this new energy for all negativity must be released as we create anew in this Thirteenth Rise of Civilization.

Through the rise of the Christed Energy within each Soul, the energy of the Christ can no longer be prevented from streaming forth through every soul and every crevice of our planet, piercing the darkness that, by the nature of Universal Law, must pass in order for the light to fulfill its existence.

Prayer

Beloved Father, we come into the Light of our existence, transcending all that we believed ourselves to be. We come to you in the full glory of this Light, of this Love that speaks so profoundly to our heart at this time. We, through our own awareness, acknowledge this great time of rapid change both on a planetary level and that of our own consciousness. We release that which no longer serves and open our hearts to receive all that You have for us.

There is no fear but only joy and love that is boundless and uplifting in this spiritual transformation we are making at this time. We are totally sub- merged in this Love of God and rejoice in the advancement of our souls at this juncture of our journey.

In our hearts and souls as we traverse forward riding the Light and Truth in Your Name, we stand in awe and complete admiration and gratitude for the full recognition of The Hand of God in all things.

Amen

CHAPTER X

———

Genesis of a New Earth

A new and extraordinary light energy is infiltrating the Earth now as many are aware as they watch the flowers bloom early or late, the seasons and weather patterns change, and seemingly strange things happen for no apparent reason. Accordingly, humanity is being affected by this new energy in the way they react to it, whether positively or negatively. Our planet, Earth is moving to a higher vibration, shifting on her axis moving to her new orbit in the galaxy in relationship with her ascension. She is reconstructing herself and life thereon is altering.

No one will be left unaffected in this wake of great change! The events of nine-eleven served as a catalyst for people to awaken, unite and discover their great love for one another. To realize that we are all connected in ways we could not possibly imagine! All is of Source! All is of the One! It matters not what you call it; *God, Father-Mother God, Allah, One, Prime Source, Creator or Universal Energy! It is what You Are!*

As we realize how connected we are, we will come to the awareness of how important each of us are in the grand design of life and how

104

important each experience is as an individual and as a collective consciousness. We tend to look at everything on our planet in duality and separation. This is an illusion! This is a preconceived idea bestowed upon us many millennia ago as a means of control.

There is not one thing on the planet or in all universes that is not part of our Creator. Thus, we are all joined together from the cohesive Love of Creation, all existence stems from Source, Divine Intelligence. *Do you realize how integral all of this is*? One aspect affects all others! As one event happens or one thought is changed, all is changed. Mankind has no perception of how powerful they are. It is a time of most importance on the planet now, a time of the most extraordinary events to have ever occurred!

Yes, what we do now and how we move forward is extremely important to all beings everywhere, whether we act from individual consciousness or as a collective planet, or even if we act at all! Thus the planet Earth is in an integral stage of her development, entering out of the darkness held so firmly in place for so many billions of years!

What is the future of this great planet that God has gifted to all Creation? Earth, Gaia, is to become the star jewel of all planets, a brilliant Sun shining brightest amidst all galaxies. Yes, Earth, Gaia, is traveling her own course now and she will be affecting great change over the coming years in her ascension process. As we are part of her, so too shall we change. Is it dramatic? Yes. Will it be easy? Not necessarily. Will it be tragic? Yes, in some instances. Will humanity be in peril? Yes, unless we change.

It is written in the annals of time this is to happen. This is but a mere dream, an illusion of linear time that was created so all souls could experience the drama of life on Earth as played out by human beings and other life forms. It matters not in the grand scheme of things, in this third dimensional time lapse that is a mere second of eternity for we are Eternal Beings. We are creations of His very Soul and our Soul lives *forever*! That is the gift of the Father, the gift of Jesus, *Eternal Life*!

This is not the end but a beginning of a New Earth, a new design of living, of creation, of Earth's loveliness ever expanding, growing, and encompassing all things. She will be newly illuminated, for she can no longer sustain herself as we know her, as we walk upon her surface, as we utilize her many gifts in a deteriorating way. She is too grand for this, too much a living organ- ism to be destroyed by our humble misgivings in abuse of her.

Gaia is like a woman who has been abused for as long as she can withstand it and now has reached the level of intolerance in which she is taking back her power, expanding in her own consciousness, and freeing herself from the constraints placed upon and within her. She is now moving to Source, changing courses and patterns within her Soul that she may live more fully from her core being. The crystals so encased within her are now freeing them- selves to the direction of their light. Thus, she can no longer be contained. In this freedom of movement she will release all negativity from the planet and from her realms of consciousness that has constrained her for these many millennia. She desires to reach her enlightened state of *Being* where she is glorious amidst all the planets and galaxies and will shine the brightest amidst them all as a consciousness of the greatest *LOVE* that ever shone, ever was, ever shall be!

This ship, planet Earth, is moving to another dimension or orbit as are all the planets in our galaxy. We are traversing with her and moving our own consciousness to a new level. It is a beautiful thing to experience this great love of Earth, her inner beauty for we are as she is! We are made of her very core being, our earth body is as her own. Thus, as we allow ourselves to be- come one with her, we shall enjoy the ride much more and be able to trust the changes taking place and know there is no ownership of anything but complete freedom.

This is the ultimate freedom, my friends. This is total Enlightenment! As we grow in Light so does she, as we grow in awareness so does she. Can you feel it, beloveds? Can you feel her love for us? Come feel her beneath your feet! Feel Gaia in the wind, in the air that you breathe, in the sunsets and the moonlit nights. Feel the *essence* of her being that is within you and stirs your soul! This is the All, the Oneness of all things! Be still. Capture this Oneness, this peace, and this love of her as we tread forward together on this incredible journey!

Come now. Experience the bliss of it! Feel the new energy that exists now on the planet for it is here to feel, to experience and partake of. It is God's Energy as gifted to us at this incredible time of change of our own state of conscious evolution. It is totally blissful if you allow it to be. Feel the expansiveness of God's Energy that radiates within and around you. It is fully supportive, and so very loving! It is more loving than anything ever experienced on the earth plane.

What a marvelous place this will be as Earth is transformed in all her beauty and magnificence, pulsating at such a high vibration, in her new level of Being. The beauty, wonders, and cities of Light will be extraordinary. Let us behold them now in our vision as they glisten and shine, radiating their love within and without. How very precious and extraordinary it is, this planet Earth to come! She is radiantly beautiful, is she not? Can you see her Majesty? Can you feel her magnificence, her love beaming to all the Universes? How brightly her light shines, how warm and loving her energy is. What an extraordinary place, home to the many that cherish her and welcome her new level of placement in the galaxies. What a treasure to behold!

We of Earth have little to imagine of this new planet, Gaia. We have no idea of what she contains within her, her magnificence, and her splendor. What wonderful gifts she holds within her living organism. What treasurers she has kept hidden from us for these many millennia, these many lifetimes. We are beholden unto her for we have not known how to use her splendid gifts. Instead, we have only misused and abused her gifts as children with a new toy, wanting to destroy them rather than find their sacredness, wanting to abuse her gifts rather than enhance and utilize them to serve us.

We are all connected, not just humanity but all living and seemingly inanimate things. All is of the One Source. At our present level of understanding, we are unable to fully grasp this concept, and, thus, we are unable to properly use the gifts of the Earth at this time. It would be folly to think that mankind has come far enough along to do otherwise but misuse these gifts of Earth, the Great Mother. They are to be exposed to us in the future that we may utilize them to benefit mankind and our new lifestyle of advancement on this natural and organic gifted planet of ours, gifted us by our Creator God.

Gaia is the most beautiful planet of all. Many would like to reside on or within her surface. Many who reside within her, who have for millennia interdimensionally, now wish to reenter the atmosphere of her exterior that they might frequent these new dimensions of life, the fourth and fifth dimensions, and beyond. They will proceed to come forward as we traverse into the fourth and fifth dimensions whereby they can be seen or discovered by this third dimension reality that is lessening now ever so silently yet ever so profoundly.

The third dimensional reality is slipping away like the waves of the ocean. This is what the Earth is experiencing now as the ebb and flow of dimensions takes place and transforms Gaia into her new life form. It is very beautiful to watch. It is a change of her Being whereby, in all respects, her life force is becoming more energetic, more geo-electric.

As she transforms, so does every man, woman, and child within her, for we are one and the same. One dances with the other and that dance is felt within all living organisms, all beings, all animal life, and all elements. Un- fettered as nature is, she too is feeling the changes with this new energy, the photon energy that is spreading like a warm blanket across her. This energy surrounds her and every living organism on and within her. It infiltrates her surface and reaches into every crevice of her being. It also infiltrates each human organism that walks upon her surface.

This new energy is of *Love* and is gifted to us at this time by God, Allah, Prime Source, Divine Intelligence in His wisdom and understanding of life force on planet Earth. This new energy is like nothing that has ever existed hereon, thus, we have no comparative pattern as humanity from which to operate. It is an extraordinary energy, a feeling of *Divine Love*. It is energy of change, a vibration or frequency like none other, one of magic, color, love, sound and instant manifestation. Is this not what God would want for His children? This God-energy is a gift for His Children to be used in a positive way, in a positive thinking manner.

This energy is not always an easy energy to focus on for it is one of great change and, thus, transformation of life as we know it. Everything will be affected by this new energy and will be transformed by it. It is very intense and many are having difficulty handling it. People are reacting to it in very strange and difficult ways, some even endangering lives. Meditation and prayer are of extreme importance now in order to stay centered, focused, and remain present amidst all the chaos and discord when our systems no longer function.

Earth is a planet of pure light and love and will be transformed into this modality as she moves on her course in the galaxy and into her new orbit.

Thus, all life on Earth must change as well. All life must let go of all the old stagnant ways and beliefs. All life must traverse into this new place decreed by God! Those who wish to journey with the Earth can do so but must now re- solve their issues and challenges regarding who they are and who they believe themselves to be.

This planet will not allow for any negativity to move forward with her nor anything created from our past lifetimes, history, belief, or understanding. The thrust will be too big to carry forth anything that does not suit Gaia now in the glory of her name and that of God and His original intent for her. She has come of age and will transform herself to her highest potential.

Now is the most pivotal time of any civilization that ever existed upon this planet. Yes, history tells us of many civilizations that have existed on earth before. This time is unprecedented. We have never before been given the gift of the opportunity to rise to such a high level of consciousness - individually, collectively, and universally.

God and the Father are one, are they not? You have heard that for many millennia. You are one with the Father! Beloveds, the Father is here with you now, this moment, if you would only trust yourself to look deep within to spend time with this part of yourself, then you would know.

You would become aware that every breath, every movement, every prayer is that of God. So listen well! What is your intent? What is your choice? You are being called now to reappraise everything you have ever been told, heard or believed!   Can you open to change?

Can you let go and fly like the eagle, spread your wings to new horizons, new thought forms, new times, new ways, new energies? You are being called forth now to do this! You are being asked by God to expand those wings and fly into new dimensions, into areas never traveled before, into new fields of thought and creation. God so loves His children in such a profound way, He now gives us the opportunity to expand ourselves into this new paradigm. We now have this glorious opportunity for birthing a new creation of peace on Earth, the peace of a thousand years foretold of this time to come, The Golden Age! Where all can learn what God's Love is all about. Now is the time, children of faith, now is the time! Do not look the other way! Do not run in fear! Stand firm, stand tall, face the God within and hear His voice calling your name for you are His Beloved. Become One with His energy, know it is there to support you, strengthen you, unfold you and love you for you are of God and God is of you!

So the new *world* and the *new order* of progression beset our planet today. It is a progression of life's existence, Prime Source, Creation, and Love for nothing can exist but out of the existence from whence all comes. This **New Earth** is of such a great consequence to the evolution of all planetary systems, and it is a vital element in the progression of all existence everywhere! It is no mere small thing we do now; rather it is of the magnificence that has been perpetuated by ourselves since we evolved here to assist Earth in her birthing process and our own. Easily done? No, just as a newborn is not brought forth easily. And yet the birth is of great perfection and joy when accomplished.

This Earth will not be recognizable as we know it today, nor shall we ourselves be recognizable as we change as radically as She. This life, as we deemed necessary for so long a period, will no longer be as we imagined but will be a mere memory of what it was during this time of history. Remnants of consciousness will remain of this time, but few will recall explicitly as to its actual existence. Similar was the case two thousand years ago when many strived to preserve its memory and recollection but none were able to do so with accuracy and conviction as to what really happened, to what is truth.

To this day, we interpret the past as we feel or see or believe it to be when, in actuality, nothing is really as it seems other than the perception of that experience at the time that it happened. Thus, how can anyone say what is truth? Is it not all conjecture after all?

What a world we will be creating in the fourth and fifth dimensions, experiencing all that is possible as we give rise to the higher levels of creation and that of Christ Consciousness. Given to us now is to be the voyagers and to bring forth this new creation of the world as we have so dreamed; that of *Heaven on Earth*. Our bodies are adjusting readily and accurately and without too much duress. Some may adjust, wondering why they don't feel well or are exceptionally tired. In truth, it is all part of the changing of the structure in which we are living, including our spiritual DNA. So be prepared for startling results when the transformation is finished within everyone!

Our third dimensional world will never be the same, so be ready to take the ride of your life. How you fare is of the greatest importance to our Creator. You must trust the process and never waver. Imagine this new world! What is your awareness about it? Can you envision it? Imagine the cities, the quality of work and the love, *the greatness of our Being*, the level of our under- standing, wholeness, sacredness, and attunement with one another. How very beautiful it is, beloveds. *How very beautiful*!

CHAPTER XI

Alpha and Omega

There is a new wave of energy now encompassing everything and causing much fluctuation of season and of weather patterns. Even people's energy levels are affected, causing them to be ungrounded and unstable. Therefore, they experience chaos and confusion and question if it is of their own doing or what else could be happening. Our scientists have a theory, but they have not yet grasped the entire concept of this evolutionary process as a major aspect of spirituality.

Climate change or Earth changes are a major factor now, as nature burns our forests, tornadoes run rampant along with floods, tsunamis, earthquakes, and other natural occurrences as wrought by nature to release the negativity so long held in her Earthly body.

Many civilizations have undergone similar times and many have not survived. Yet, so many more today understand more fully the circumstances that are surrounding shifting energy patterns. We will find much change on our planet in every area possible for the portals of change are in our midst. This is what is transpiring now energetically. We are at a crossroads in time and space.

Thus, in our third dimension there are voluminous misconceptions and perspectives being laid as groundwork to keep us under the control of those who have so misguided us for many billions of years, eons actually. This is why we have had great Messiah's come to the planet—Buddha, Krishna, Mohammad, Jesus, and others—to assist in bringing change to the conscious field, to change the vibration of thinking that has been tribal and a stronghold keeping us in the dark and out of the evolution of all the other galaxies.

Now is the time for the misguided souls to realize they no longer have control and must succeed to the light or they will be lost in this warring of the light and dark. A time is coming when all will be cast in a dead shadow or darkness so vast that people will not see the hand in front of them. Each will be surrounded in this darkness and will be challenged on a subatomic level as to who they really are and what their beliefs are—not the beliefs of others but those of their own soul.

The time is rapidly coming for this to take place as our planet changes her axis and enters the photon energy belt, gamma ray, portal-black hole whereby all existence will be changed forever. There will not be a hair on one's head that is not affected by this darkness or light as the case may be for all consciousness will be changed forever and what we know of as third dimensional life will cease to be. All will be in great turmoil as much damage is done, and many will be departing. People will remain thinking they are third dimensional when, in reality, another dimensional shift will have occurred. This darkness will be global and unparalleled in all the course of planetary history. It will afford such a change in vibration for humanity and on the planet itself. The vibration alone will create havoc even for those who are able to carry it to the new level by becoming one with it.

By accepting the love of our Creator and having an understanding as to what is actually taking place, you will be able to withstand the changes better, to be consciously aware that a new evolutionary process is taking place. You will once and for all be totally connected to your soul's vibration and to God, and you will know it! This knowledge will either propel you forward in fear or allow you to see vistas of yourself you have not known before or of which you have never been aware.

The darkness, or the light, will bring you closer to God than you have ever been. Indeed, you will be forced to look within to your own subatomic structure. In this awareness, you will be unable to see or feel outside of yourself as the cocoon of darkness or light envelops you. Those who have followed and recognized their spiritual path will not have the same difficulty as others who have not for they will be surrounded by the Light of the Christ and will be held in a cocoon of loving energy, immersed in love and at peace through this period of time. They will be open to the light in such a way that they can provide assistance for those who will need help after the reemergence of all. There will be those who are sought out for healing, for information, and security that the world is not destructing.

I encourage you to accept these words as truth and to realize your potential here on Earth, to realize what a gift Mother Earth is to each of us as we become more open to God, to life, and to our own spiritual journeys. This will lessen the impact of this time period on our planet. Otherwise, more destruction will follow. Your choice is always given to you as you believe. This is Divine Law, thus it has to be.

The magnetic shift will alter all the normal perception we live with on a daily basis and the infrastructure of life will be radically shaken and changed. As we reemerge from this darkness or light, it will seemingly appear that we are one and the same with hardly a memory of the previous situation. But there will be a considerable difference. We will know on a cellular level that something has transpired, and there we will find the truth of who we are.

Many will say it is the work of Satan. Many will think it is the coming end of time according to prophecies in the Bible. Many of our pastors and ministers will think they have been right and claim credit for this change, a product of their preaching.

The spiritual archives are rich with material never shared with us human species on our planet. Much was hidden from mankind to keep people under control and locked in the reality of tribal consciousness. This has got to stop. As the new paradigm unfolds, new realities, whereby the old understanding, as taught by tribal beliefs, will no longer exist.

Changes are so swiftly taking place in every area of life as we know it so swiftly that we, as a human race or populace, can't seem to keep up with it all. Chaos reigns around the world as all feel the same stress of having to do too much in order to keep abreast of life's fast pace. This compression of time has never occurred to such a degree as it is now. And this creates a sort of free fall as it moves ever increasingly faster, collapsing in on itself. Many feel like nothing is stable and there is nothing left to grasp. The unfamiliarity of this phenomenon intensifies the human psyche to react in distress. The brain, being a computer data bank, has nothing to register this against, and this creates more uncertainty and chaos rather than allowing for what is.

Life will, quite simply, be as an untold magnificence. Life will be in the radiance and splendor of the Garden that once was there for us to play in as children. That has been the Father's gift to us all along, to be as children and to experience all that *is*, all that He has for us, and all that is now coming to the fore. That Garden is ours in the formidable moment of the NOW; to be- hold, to experience, and to play in would we but choose this for ourselves.

We have never seen a garden so beautiful, so rich in all the senses of our embodiments, a place where the sun shines constantly and the Earth is a radiant expression of the light. We are expressions of this Earth for as she is so are we. Thus, the splendor of all will be a majestic and radiant beauty. There will be no room for negativity, and the shadows of another time will disappear as the splendor of the Creator's work shines forth. All will be made known to mankind, and the wealth stored for the human race will be part of our every- day existence.

The richness of life will be there for us to partake of in the sacredness of what has been preserved for our new consciousness, our new ways of living, thinking, and being. Soon, the shackles will be cleared from our minds and the darkness will transform itself into the light. Each soul will recognize itself no longer as that of duality but rather will return to the essence of that which it is and will be a perfected soul to such a heightened degree that all will resemble the power of our Creator. In the cosmic seas of energy, one lifetime follows another as one's soul is always in constant movement and growth patterns, encasing all that is possible for it to know and experience in this Earth school and that of other worlds.

There will be a time of resurgence of such magnitude that all that is familiar will cease to be. Thus, will be formed the new beginnings, the New Jerusalem, The Golden Age that was promised by our Creator at this time of evolution. It will be an age of all that is possible and all that is rich and beautiful in Divine Grace of the Father's blessings on Earth!

Indeed, we cannot reach such a state of evolution without the transitory state of rapture, of cleansing, of purging and removing all that does not work. And so, for this great movement for change, this great surge in the full sweeping motion of the photon energy is upon the planet now and causing this great change and challenge to be manifest. Civilizations have had this same type of energy in the past, yet not to the degree it encompasses Earth now nor to the extent of the grids changing so dramatically. We have not had the capabilities to hold the grids in place, thus, it was never possible to overlay them in such a manner.

Now, we are assisted by beings on the other side in the overlay process of this great change of life force, a new subatomic structure being created within the embodiment of our being. This is done without our full awareness

on Earth but on a spiritual level, and it is already being accomplished by those Beings who love us and wish to see us remain on the planet. In order to function in the new energy, we must match this level of vibration or we will cease to exist. All the Angels and Ascended Masters will be present to walk beside us, to share their wealth and ours on an equal footing.

The rays of the Great Central Sun pour energy through all realms of Earth, through all beings and life forms thereon. This energy is pouring forth now, breathing new life into her. These are energies that cause her to no longer succumb to that which she has held to herself for so long a time now, in support of life on Earth.

Planet Earth, as the other planetary systems, is evolving and rotating differently and moving into a new position in orbit to allow other planets to come forward, moving out of the cradle they have held for so long. The sun will be much closer to the Earth and the atmosphere will be very different. Likewise, our bodies will be lighter and more radiant. This will accommodate the new energies of Earth easier and will give us the mobility we need to move, being transported by thought rather than machine if we so choose.

Indeed, the planet is undergoing a transformation of phenomenal changes such as have never been witnessed in the total existence of her Being. She will be so transformed that not a grain of sand will be left untouched nor a mountain peak nor drop of water in the ocean. As she swings on her axis to the opposite direction, the Antarctic rotating up toward the Arctic, her core essence will also shift and she will rotate in the opposite direction. This will cause seasons to change and the lessening of time as we know it.

During this process, we too, as human life on this planet, will change within our own planetary system of embodiment, as we are doing now in or- der to accommodate new spheres of energies and shifts. We are witnesses and participants in the birth of a new creation of living and being. We are walking closer with God in our own rightful divine self. We are recognizing that aspect of who we are and taking back that which is rightfully ours by His Grand Design, which is our birthright gifted by our Creator.

The misappropriation of man's thought and will have led to much destruction and abuse of our beloved planet Earth, and she reclaims herself now at this juncture for her own expansion and existence. To maintain that of who and what she is as a living organism, she too extends herself to a higher level of vibration, that she might be consciously more aware of the Creator and all life that resides upon her belly.

As she is rocked out of her orbit and spins to the opposite side of her current rotation, much will change and many will consciously and or unconsciously make the choice to leave, to journey to the other side. Some will remain with the new planet Earth, as it will thus be inhabited, though none will be allowed to remain on Gaia unless they are of the light and rooted in the Great I AM (God). Her energy will be so extraordinary and to such a degree that unless our human energy is compatible with hers, we will not be able to sustain ourselves in her new atmosphere and sphere of rotation.

Dramatically and in full Presence, she will take this turn on her axis. She will move into her new orbit, and she will expand her landmasses. She will take the necessary steps to cleanse herself of all the warring and bloodshed upon her bosom, the killing of each other and the negativity, untruths, and non-sustaining life forms that have perpetuated her destruction. Whether it is a conscious or unconscious decision by you, it will be made on a Soul level, and your decision will create for you a new level of understanding of life, love, and the *Truth* of who you really are.

Now comes the day when exciting things shall transpire on the planet and we will witness many things as never before experienced or seen. The new evolution of man will afford the opportunity to advance to a greater and deeper level of consciousness, that of the Chirst-Conciousness and thus opens realities that were impossible before.

Our cosmic brethren have held to the fore until this time when we would be able to hold the new energy. They await us and ask that we honor them for much depends on our process as to their own evolution. The higher we progress, they too will benefit in reaching higher evolutions. They are here to assist us in the perilous times ahead. We are not to render them our enemy out of controlled fear through mass media nor the many fear-based movies of the past. Rather, we will be very grateful to these cosmic Beings who are as we and have come to assist in the perilous time upon Earth.

So there is much strife now on the planet that will continue to intensify for a period of time. Those who are causing such strife have much unrest and discomfort with their lot in life. They are in deep rage within themselves with little hope for change. Rather than examine their own choices, they will cast blame on all those they deem responsible.

In truth, all have chosen their roles for this particular time and all are operating on a soul level to clear that which they have carried energetically for many lifetimes. Humans are up for review. Now is the time for the great clearing of the human race and those who have done much harm on the planet, those who have controlled the masses for a very long time. The truth will be opened wide soon for us to know how very much we have been manipulated and used for centuries. Much upheaval will be caused not only on the planet in her earth changes but in the minds of humans who have been so misled to believe that which is not true.

The Earth will undergo all that is necessary to cleanse her of the negativity that has been instilled within her Being for all these many millennia. All negativity shall be erased and a New Earth shall emerge, one full of beauty, love, joy and peace for those who reside thereon. The planet will provide a new environment to inhabit in the future. Many souls await to inhabit this New Earth to reveal in her sanctity and beauty. Those who travel with her during this transition will be the precursors of this new life on the planet for the next one thousand years, a place of safe keeping where the Garden of Eden will be the grandest Gift of God in His Benevolence for His children.

We come to you this day, Beloved God, in full awareness of our choice to elevate our Christ-Consciousness to that of your Grand Design for us. We recognize our Source and our strength at a time of unprecedented change upon our beloved Earth and within our core being.

All is as it should be in the greatness of Your Majesty's Grand Design for humanity and all life. We accept ourselves for who we truly are and surround ourselves in the Light of the Christ as we engage in this transitory process of evolution of our beloved Earth and our being birthed anew.

I AM THAT I AM. *AMEN.*

· · · ·

None will stray from the flock again, but all will regain the majesty that was forfeited so many millennia previously. Men and women will be balanced within themselves as the male and female of each soul. The God and Goddess will reunite within themselves.

Now, we are forging for humankind new parallels, new dynamics for all!

The cosmic wave of energies will create a means of living in total and complete balance within each person's soul without the parlay of male and female or the dominance of one over the other.